CLAIMING NEW LIFE

CLAIMING NEW LIFE

Process-Church
for the Future

LISA R. WITHROW

LUCAS PARK BOOKS

BOOKS
ST. LOUIS, MISSOURI

Biblical quotations, unless otherwise noted, are from the *New Revised Standard Version Bible,* copyright 1989, Division of Christian Education of the National Council of Churches of Christ in the USA. Used by permission.

ISBN: 9781603500470

Published by Lucas Park Books

www.lucasparkbooks.com

Originally published by Chalice Press.

Printed in the United States of America

Contents

Acknowledgments

As the daughter of an ordained clergywoman, I have known what it means to be part of the church all of my life. As an ordained clergywoman myself, I have faced the joys and tribulations of leadership in the parish, where I have learned much over fourteen years of commitment. My doctoral work examined the future of the church as long ago as the late 1980s and I have been watching the changes unfold ever since. Now my students, who are negotiating theological school, face that future; my hope is that they claim their own authority to lead the church through its current wilderness into a new era of wholeness and love.

My gratitude goes to the churches who have helped shape my thinking and also to colleagues at Methodist Theological School in Ohio who help me examine the life of the church through the eyes of their different disciplines. I am grateful to colleagues and friends who bolstered me during both the inception and subsequent writing of *Claiming New Life*. In particular, The Rev. Sandy Selby offered her wisdom and words for this endeavor. Finally, I am blessed to be surrounded by a support network of intelligent readers and life-giving encouragers who touch base with me regularly about teaching and writing. They are true community, always ready for the adventure ahead.

Introduction

The notion of process spans a variety of disciplines and fields of study. Business leaders speak of cycles, processes, and systems as they describe the movement of organizations. Biologists talk about organic processes by which organisms interact and ecosystems evolve. Physicists attempt to demonstrate the process of matter reorganizing itself with greater complexity each time it is thrown into chaos. Therapists study systems of behavior and processes by which people interact and grow. Historians and sociologists note cycles of events and accompanying human proclivities in cultures through the process of time. Educators speak about learning processes. Biblical scholars and theologians point out the processes of thought and explanation through which human beings move to try to understand God in relation to creation.

Claiming New Life: Process-Church for the Future invites those who care deeply about the church to move into an intentional process of co-creating the future of the church with God. The church has evolved over millennia; in a sense, it has always been in process. The endeavor introduced here invokes an intentional choice for the church to live into its future through a process-based lens, while remaining rooted in tradition and mindful of its present context.

When the Christian community learns to understand itself as responding to God's call to be co-creators of the future, it engages in process thought as a way to understand church. *Claiming New Life* relies on process theology to introduce a process ecclesiology or, in this volume, "The Process-Church," as a particular way for community to be faithful to God's call. Attention to post-Christendom, postmodern, globalizing elements sets the context for Process-Church development. Methods to introduce communities to living as Process-Church are accompanied by discussion about transitions from static to process-oriented mindsets. Finally, illustrations of process work in churches set in different types of venues exemplify the potential that Process-Church brings to the future of the church.[1]

What is process ecclesiology? "Ecclesiology" is derived from *ekklesia,* a Greek word meaning "assembly" or "gathering." More accurately, *ek* (out of) and *kalein* (called) signify "a gathering of those called out of." Ecclesiology then is the theological understanding of the nature and mission of the church as a gathering of people called out by God to particular purposes. For Christians, this definition raises the question, called out from what and for what? One answer is to claim that Christians are called out by Christ to be free *from* bondage.[2] The content of the call is to live in and *for* radical love in the realm of God, based on the great commandment.[3] By implication, Christians will not live into the realm of God if the faithful stay within the structures and systems of society and the bonds of private existence.

Add "process" to "ecclesiology," and the nature of being a gathering called out of bondage to proclaim wholeness[4] and love shifts from institutional function to intentional co-creation of the future with God. Process promotes a sense of living into an unfolding realm in which people participate with God to bring about God's purposes. Thus, "process ecclesiology" is an organic understanding of Christians gathered for the purposes of partnering with God to live in freedom and bring wholeness and love to the world.

Claiming New Life begins by naming the contexts in which process ecclesiology, more practically called Process-Church, finds its calling. To introduce Process-Church requires looking at a significant question before the mainline church in the current era: how can the mainline church claim new life based on wholeness and love in a postmodern, globalizing world where many understandings of truth constitute faith? This question spurred the thinking behind *Claiming New Life* because it is a question on the lips of parishioners throughout the Western world.[5] Developing Process-Church, a practical process ecclesiology that claims tradition and, at the same time, evolves into God's purpose for the future in a new way, is one approach to address this vital question. The focus of this volume provides cultural, theological, and practical bases for initiating Process-Church.

Part One introduces theological, social, geographic, and economic circumstances in which mainline churches currently function. The first four chapters describe social locations of the church, which ultimately finds itself in the wilderness. Surrounded by post-Christendom, globalizing, and postmodern influences, the church often does not know which way to turn.

Chapter 1 introduces Corner Church as a mainline congregation facing decline. The questions before Corner Church illustrate a sense of a congregation wandering in the wilderness, hoping for a meaningful future without a means to get there. Corner Church will provide an example in chapter 6 for becoming Process-Church as its leadership works through the scenario-building process outlined there.

Chapter 2 establishes the premise that God's love for creation and the corresponding response of creation to God is the foundational relationship for all life. The role of the church is to be the body of God's incarnational love as it has been made known to Christians in Christ Jesus. The chapter identifies a significant question before the church as the body of Christ struggles to find its place in a post-Christendom, globalizing world. This struggle has promoted anxiety in churches throughout Western societies, with responses that often do not further the role of the church in meaningful ways.

Chapter 3 explores the contexts in which the mainline church finds itself by discussing the impact of the global influence on the local community and the local influence on the global community. Globalizing forces affect communities in both helpful and damaging ways.

Chapter 4 continues to set the stage for the work of the church by exploring the meanings of a hard-to-define word, *postmodern*. Descriptions of the emerging church movement provide one significant illustration of postmodern Christian communities in this age. Each of the chapters in Part One contributes to the contextual foundation from which a different way of claiming new life for the mainline church can emerge, beginning with Corner Church.

Part Two invites churches to claim new life by developing an understanding of process theology, which in turn leads to developing a process ecclesiology or, in common parlance, a "Process-Church." Discussion of the elements necessary for the church to become faithful people on a journey in a complex, rapidly changing world provides the focus for this section. Some elements of Process-Church echo the claims of the emerging church movement, while alternatively placing value on tradition and a theological understanding that the church is the extension of God's incarnation: the church is God's hands in the world. Process-Church embraces what emerges, but also casts an intentionally self-critical eye on its own role in co-creating a future of wholeness and love. Process-Church incorporates an ethic of inquiry to participate intentionally in its unfolding future while claiming the value of transcendent experiences of God.

Chapter 5 discusses theoretical and theological foundations for developing a "Process-Church," arguing that church-in-process provides a flexible, relevant means by which the great commandment can be shared in a rapidly changing world. Chapter 6 introduces a systematic method called scenario-building by which churches can imagine their futures and live as Process-Churches that constantly reinvent themselves as they respond to the world with a prophetic message of wholeness and love. Here, Corner Church is reintroduced from chapter 1 as an example of how the congregation can move from Institutional Church to Process-Church.

Part Three integrates the great hope for the church in the midst of a complex world (Part One) with the theological foundations and inquiry required to develop Process-Church (Part Two). Moving from foundational claims about the mainline church's role in the midst of challenging contexts to living faithfully in a new way as part of God's creation requires attention to transitional concerns. Transition calls for leaders who are capable of accompanying people on the journey into and through the wilderness, transforming community to bring new life and wholeness to the world.

Chapter 7 describes the theological and practical shifts needed in congregational life for transitional work from Institutional Church to Process-Church to be effective. Attention to caring for congregations living in the wilderness is important for times of change. Often chaos emerges as an element of change in the wilderness. Congregations can negotiate the chaos if hope remains present in the wilderness journey. Chapter 8 introduces specific areas important for leaders who invite congregations to become Process-Churches. Leaders themselves need to develop their own disciplines to allow for healthy, meaningful transitions in the church.

Part Four illustrates the contextual and methodological components of churches living into process orientations. In this section imagining becoming a Process-Church invites the church into claiming new life in the hope of wholeness for creation. Love for God and for neighbor motivates churches to share the good news of this hope. The body of Christ, living into a new age, learns to be flexible and attentive to social, economic, environmental, and spiritual needs that lie beyond consumerism. In chapter 9, four existing mainline church settings, each in some form of decline, are introduced. Theological reflection and scenario-building exercises in each of these settings provide examples for transforming churches from anxious institutions to Process-Churches, promoting a relevant message of hope and love for the world.

Descriptions for each church have been generalized so that they represent "types" of churches rather than specific congregations. These descriptions provide a snapshot of the setting. Emphasis is placed on the scenario-building process as a means to becoming Process-Church rather than exploring congregational and leadership dynamics.

Chapter 10 draws together the initial question facing the mainline church with the development of the Process-Church as a means to engage the question faithfully as response to it evolves. Process-Church ultimately focuses on co-creating with God the unfolding future based in the commandment to love God, self, and neighbor.

Claiming New Life surveys a wide range of topics such as globalization, post-Christendom, postmodernism, and process theology. Each topic requires study beyond the scope of this book for a deeper understanding of its complexities and nuances. The introductory remarks found in chapters here serve to lay basic groundwork for the development of Process-Church.

Finding new life for the mainline church is no easy task. The proposal in this volume requires discipline and long-term commitment with a constant and continual grounding in God's purposes. No "quick fix" checklist exists in these pages. Instead, the requirements for mainline transformation call people who love the church to develop a learning posture, open and risk-oriented, in conjunction with fortitude for living productively in the wilderness for a time. Process-Church development is not for the faint of heart. Rather, it is a process for those who yearn to reconnect with God's present-future desires based on radical love in the midst of a complex, often destructive world.

PART I

Setting the Scene

1

Corner Church

Utopia's most pronounced characteristic is a limited and contained community in which the potential of the individual as well as that of the society can be actualized.

HOWARD THURMAN[1]

Existing mainline churches reside in a wide variety of sociopolitical and economic contexts. Mainline churches that have been established for more than ten years have a particular set of concerns that differ from house-based churches or new churches. Established congregations have formed habits and assumptions in their life together that make an impact on their self-understanding and their approaches to ministry. Those churches that experience decline or simply maintain themselves face a more difficult task regarding ministry effectiveness than new church communities.

Corner Church represents one such declining church. The simple description below serves to introduce a setting not atypical of many churches found in the Western world. The overarching questions facing Corner Church are important for most established churches. The concerns specific to the church's setting also deserve particular attention. Each chapter following this description addresses the factors that affect churches, some like Corner Church and others set in different contexts. Corner Church will be revisited in chapter 6 as an illustration of how it might live into its future as Process-Church through a scenario-building method.

Corner Church

Corner Church, established in 1973, was built at the crossroads of two lower middle-class suburban townships near an urban center. The urban center itself is considered to be part of the "rust belt," where the steel industry has abandoned its manufacturing plants for more lucrative markets overseas. Unemployment rates are high, and abandoned steel plants dot the local landscape.

Corner Church finds itself surrounded by six other churches. The nearest denominational affiliate churches are two and four miles away in opposite directions, each in the heart of more affluent suburban cultures. One of these neighboring churches is well-established with a long-term pastoral leader and averages 645 attendees on any given Sunday; this church considers itself stable. The other has a new, charismatic minister and is growing by forty or more members per year, averaging four hundred on Sundays. Four additional independent churches are located within one mile of Corner Church. They are similar in size and context to Corner Church, and all claim sixty to one-hundred attendees on Sundays, with little or no change in these numbers during the past two decades.

Corner Church sits on two acres of land in a neighborhood where small, single-story homes were built in the 1950s. The majority of families in the neighborhood have lived most of their lives in the community, though their grown children no longer remain in the area. One part of the neighborhood merges into a high-crime area with a reputation for high turnover in the housing market, drug trafficking, and "crack houses." Corner Church understands itself to be one of the havens for its neighborhood, particularly in light of the encroaching rising criminal activity on one border.

Another section of the neighborhood shares property boundaries with a local park, including walking trails and a public golf course. Large suburban homes border the golf course, and a local builder would like to acquire more land to expand the development. Corner Church is part of this transitional area.

On Sundays, Corner Church can count on seventy regular attendees, doubling that number on Christian festival days such as

Christmas and Easter, or when the church offers public meals after worship. Attendees constitute a multicultural demographic, including people of Mexican, Lebanese, and European backgrounds. The minister at Corner Church, Rev. Jamie, is ordained, claims thirteen years of experience in parish ministry, and holds a Master of Divinity degree. He is Caucasian with eastern European ancestry.

The sanctuary at Corner Church can seat two hundred people in a light-filled room with custom-made communion table, pulpit, and lectern. Worship blends a variety of musical traditions with emphasis on the denominational hymnal's offerings. Rev. Jamie celebrates communion monthly; he invites congregational participation in worship every Sunday by writing short dramas and coaching liturgists. Rev. Jamie's primary focus at Corner Church is worship and program development that addresses neighborhood needs.

Corner Church has a talented volunteer and paid staff leadership team, mostly female, all retired from teaching or blue- and pink-collar positions in local industry or small business. Structures of authority remain informal. No identifiable matriarch or patriarch runs the church, though there are several strong influencers in the leadership team. Decision-making is highly participatory, with emphasis on how choices affect internal relationships and financial status. Corner Church commits itself yearly to balancing its budget and finding ways to raise money for causes outside its own church walls. Congregants are as generous as they can be on fixed incomes and tight personal budgets.

Most members of Corner Church have known each other for several decades and share daily life together with church activities as their social foundation. Of ultimate concern to members is Corner Church's ability to care for each other. Rev. Jamie is considered a part of the church family because he attends to pastoral care regularly, particularly with aging congregants. Some members anonymously contribute money and time to others when there is need. The generous spirit of the church stems from a piety introduced by the founding minister of the congregation and an understanding of the community "pulling together" in an increasingly economically challenged area. However, the financial and volunteer resource base for Corner Church continues to decline rapidly as members die and few new faces are seen on Sundays other than visiting extended family.

Corner Church's unique ministry at one time constituted neighborhood outreach to children whose parents were not available after school. "Missing" parents, as the after-school church leadership group called them, included those who were involved in the drug trade, addicts themselves, or those who had to work several jobs to make ends meet. Through a preschool program, church members identified children who were raising their own brothers and sisters in poverty. They also noted that children were playing in the parking lot and occasionally ringing the church doorbell to "find out what was going on in there." Teachers extended their program to an after-school structured playtime. They collected clothing, shoes, and food for the children, who would wander over to the church when they wished to or when in need. Behavioral challenges and medical needs added another layer to the after-school program early in its inception. Teachers themselves underwent training for working with special needs children.

After a decade of this work, the teachers began to show signs of burnout. The lead teacher indicated that she had been thinking about retirement from the program for at least three years but could not bring herself to "leave the children" without a source of support. No new teachers or volunteers were putting themselves forward, however, and the workload had been increasing every year. Rev. Jamie recognized the commitment level of the teachers as well as the inordinate amount of time and energy required to address the growing needs of the children in the neighborhood. He did not know what the next step might be other than to invite overloaded, understaffed social agencies to become involved. Within two years, the teachers retired and the program dwindled and eventually dissolved. The leadership team continues to attend church regularly, but few children are present in worship or during the week. The aging congregation itself gives generously to people in need but does not have the energy to work on their behalf any longer.

Questions Facing Corner Church

Corner Church members grieve the loss of a ministry they have identified as vital for the local community. Rev. Jamie is looking for a new way of being in ministry that addresses the already-identified challenges faced by children and families in the area. Corner Church pays attention to neighborhood children and growing crime rates and feels helpless in the midst of these concerns. A spiritual wilderness becomes increasingly evident for Corner Church as it acknowledges that it does not have the human or financial resources to retain the ministry it knows it is called to have in the neighborhood. Particular questions arise for a church wandering in this wilderness of lost dreams and hopes.

In this current state, how can Corner Church address the question about claiming new life based on wholeness and love in a postmodern, globalizing world where many understandings of truth constitute faith? How does Corner Church begin to understand the social and economic factors affecting the neighborhood and, subsequently, the church itself? What does living the good news of radical love mean for Corner Church, and how might the congregation do so with limited resources and an uncertain future?

These questions signify the issues facing mainline churches today while also addressing the concerns of a particular church setting. The next five chapters speak to the questions above. By introducing a foundational focus on the great commandment as churches wander in the wilderness of decline, the basis for Christian life and work together becomes clear. Further, defining contexts in which these churches find themselves, and proposing a process for claiming new life that invites the people of God to join God in the co-creation of the future, provides a method for becoming Process-Church. Corner Church will reappear in chapter 6 to show how it can address the questions facing it in a way that brings hope for the future.

2

The Great Hope

All the church has ever needed to rise from the dead is memory,
bread, wine and Holy Spirit—that, and care for the world
that is at least equal to her care for her own preservation.
Where church growth has eclipsed church depth, it is possible to
hear very little about the world except as a rival for the human
resources needed by the church for her own survival.

BARBARA BROWN TAYLOR[1]

Those who have experience with mainline churches will
understand Barbara Brown Taylor's reference to anxiety about church
survival. Years of steadily declining numbers have taken their toll on
congregations and clergy.[2] Taylor herself chose to leave the parish
ministry after fourteen years of service as an Episcopal priest. Those
who choose to stay in leadership find that it can be costly. They
often find themselves exhausted by congregational conflict, high
expectations of parishioners, and chronic anxiety.

Others choose different avenues of ministry altogether, a growing
trend particularly among young adults. They do not wish to be leaders
in a conflicted, declining institution. A survey conducted by the Lewis
Center for Christian Leadership indicates that people under the age
of thirty-five constitute only 6 percent or less of the ordained clergy
serving in the mainline denominations. Actual numbers show that

each mainline denomination in the United States has between two hundred and nine hundred young clergy in parishes at this time.[3] Further, the Alban Institute reports that mainline churches have fewer theological students of any age entering parish ministry than twenty years ago.[4]

The church itself was born out of conflict and a small group of leaders. Mark's gospel tells how Jesus met with opposition from the beginning of his ministry, enduring confrontation by religious authorities and hometown neighbors. After his final entry into Jerusalem, the conflict escalated in the public square, leading ultimately to his crucifixion. It was in the midst of this conflict in Jerusalem that the basis for a new covenant community began to unfold. During his ministry Jesus named two commandments, calling his followers back to the basic confession of faith, the purpose for which they were created: to love.

The Great Commandment

In Luke, a lawyer tests Jesus. In Matthew, a Pharisee does the same. In Mark 12:28–32, a scribe approaches Jesus after witnessing Jesus' success with Sadducees who had just tested his wisdom. In fact, Jesus already had spent a portion of his day responding to challenges from several groups holding power in Jerusalem: chief priests and scribes (Mk. 11:28), Pharisees and Herodians (Mk. 12:13), and the Sadducees (Mk. 12:23). These challenges included questions about his authority, education, and theology. Jesus rendered his opponents speechless, dishonoring them in public, as the scribe would have noticed.

In verse 28, Mark's scribe enters, but his motives are unclear. He simply asks, "Which commandment is the first of all?" The question stems from a desire to know what principle Jesus would choose from among the more than six hundred precepts summarized by scribes and rabbis in codifying the law.[5] In verses 29–30, Jesus answers by essentially quoting Deuteronomy 6:4–5 (the *Shema*): "The LORD is our God, the LORD alone. You shall love the LORD your God with all your heart, and with all your soul, and with all your might." By answering the scribe this way, Jesus confirms that he stands in Jewish tradition. But he inserts one phrase in Mark 12:30: "with all your mind." Reference to the *Shema* would impress the Jews because the verses are the most treasured verses of Judaism, emphasizing the sovereignty of God in all areas of life.[6] Then Jesus concludes with Leviticus 19:18b, loving neighbor as self, thereby showing his wide knowledge of the sacred texts. Unique to Mark is the final statement: "There is no other commandment greater than these" (Mk. 12:31). Matthew's version indicates that all other laws grow out of these two (Mt. 22:40).

The scribe in Mark's gospel repeats back to Jesus what he just heard and increases the two greatest commandments' importance by claiming that they surpass whole burnt offerings and sacrifices (Hos. 6:6). The scribe affirms Jesus' remarks and continues the conversation, indicating his respect for Jesus publicly. Then Jesus notes that the scribe has answered wisely, loving God with his mind as well as heart, soul, and strength.

The onlookers say nothing more after this exchange. They had just witnessed competition and challenge changing to acceptance; Jesus declared the scribe being close to the realm of God (Mk. 12:34). The inquiry initiated by the scribe led him to a deeper faith, a deeper knowledge of the purpose of God to which Jesus pointed. Followers of Jesus, the community of believers, also were finding new ways to be faithful as they asked questions. Ultimately, Jesus drew them and all who would listen back to the basis for community: love of God and neighbor with all one's being.

The function of this story is to present a central doctrine of early Gentile Christianity. "Righteousness is not to be understood as strict obedience to a complex code of laws and customs. The one commandment that is central is the principle of love."[7] The dual command of love offers Mark's community a way of presenting the core of their faith and heritage to others. This great commandment still calls followers to give their whole lives—heart, soul, mind, and strength—to be grounded in the love of God and neighbor. God calls forth all creation to live into this love and wholeness.

God's creative power works in the world by luring all of God's creation toward God's purpose. God gave humanity the gift of stewardship for creation, God's hands in the world. Human beings are to be co-creators with God, with all activity aimed toward God's purpose, wholeness, and love. This is why the great commandment summarizes the mission to which Christ calls the church. The church, to be faithful, constantly must renew and refresh its grounding in the love of God, and Christ's church must love the neighbor to whom it is connected through God's love.

In Luke, Jesus told the parable of the good Samaritan to define "neighbor" to his followers (Lk. 10:25–37). In this case, neighbor was a man whom the Jews deemed racially impure and religiously heretical who nonetheless helped a wounded man when religious leaders did not. Jesus challenged the definition of neighbor by focusing on the "how" rather than "who" in this parable. The commandment in this story is clear: show love to those who need it, no matter who they are.

Throughout history, the church has struggled to love its neighbor. The mainline church of the twenty-first century has become inwardly focused, caring for neighbors absentmindedly or not at all. Those churches that do pay attention to the world outside their doors often struggle with living out the great commandment in a diverse, rapidly changing, multicultural world.

Luke, having shown how one loves neighbor, follows by showing how one loves God (Lk. 10:38–42). Martha invites Jesus to her home, where she and Mary host Jesus and the disciples. Martha remains busy with hospitality while Mary sits at the feet of Jesus to learn from him. This listening and learning proves to be holy space, *temenos*,[8] and time, *kairos*,[9] where Jesus reveals the nature of God and where Mary responds by her attentiveness.

In many ways the church itself has become inattentive. Its disconnection with God's call stems from a preoccupation with its perceived status. However, this uncertain territory, a wilderness of sorts, is hardly new for the people of God. They have found themselves in wilderness before. Hebrew narratives include rebellion and redemption, captivity and deliverance. All these narratives portray wilderness times when God's people turned away and did not attend to God's purposes. The "murmuring stories" of Exodus and Numbers[10] tell of a delivered people who deal with the wilderness uncertainty by longing to return to the past, even a painful past, because at least it was familiar.

Yet in the wilderness God lifts up unexpected leaders who, though inarticulate and flawed, have precisely the qualities God's people needed: faithfulness, integrity, vulnerability, and willingness to risk everything for God.[11] In the wilderness, God provides water and manna.[12] In the wilderness, God prepares Jesus for his ministry.[13] In the wilderness, God calls the church to new life and new hope. God created persons through love and for love; love for each other and for all of God's creation. Thus, the church's mission is to be a people attentive to God's constant call to move toward wholeness and love by embodying its stories and bringing hope to neighbors around the world.

The Wilderness

The biblical writers tell humanity that, in creating the world, God ordered the chaos. God did not eliminate it, but shaped it in creative tension.[14] It is in this tension between order and chaos that the church finds itself, often in wilderness, desiring order for comfort. The fearsome nature of wilderness often led to discontent, and still does today. Yet the pursuit of comfort or the avoidance of chaos denies human beings full participation in the gifts of the wilderness experience.

Christianity holds that God became incarnate in Jesus Christ to redeem a world that had lost its way and to show human beings how to relate to one another, live in love, and work as co-creators with God. The church is the extension of the incarnation of Christ, calling the world to redemption through wholeness and love.

Christ himself commissioned followers to go into the world and bring people to God; the great work of the disciples was to carry out this commission to bring all to wholeness and love. This commission remains steadfast as a call for the church, inviting humanity to know the love of God for all creatures and to live out that love with all of one's being.

Through the course of history, when the institutional church has not been able to live up to this calling, God has brought about new life and new perspectives, either from within the church or through new ways of expressing the faith. The early pre-Constantinian church was a radical expression of faithful life, running quickly into tension with authorities. However, the conversion of Constantine and the imperialization of the church resulted in exponential growth and success, as defined by the world. The early church's stories of sacrifices and risks for the sake of the faith became less important for the politically sanctioned church.[15]

Christians live now in post-Constantinian times, where the good news is as foreign to the world and its establishments as it was to the world in which Jesus lived. People of the church find themselves in a wilderness as frightening as the desert in which the Hebrew people walked after leaving Egypt. Like many in the early stages of the exodus, churches seem to want to go back to what is familiar, but there is urgency not to do so. If Moses' followers had turned back, they never would have found the land of promise. Outside the church there is a wilderness as well. The broken world puts humanity in a state of crisis that can be both destructive and generative. Who other than the church has stories of hope in the wilderness, stories of new life in brokenness?

Thus, the church calls forth growth in the wilderness. Bringers of salvation come from dryness, from the desert, and from barren places. People may lead barren lives, thirsting for meaning, but yet know about hope: Sarah laughs, Zechariah believes, and Jesus brings living water. Christians make the definition of the church's work complicated, but it remains simple. God created humanity in love, for love, for each other, for all of God's creation. Thus, the church's mission is to be a people open to God's constant lure toward wholeness and love. Those who have the courage to speak prophetically about ways through the wilderness admit the need that human beings have for new paths, the hard work of transformation and redemption that must be done. For anyone who lives, moves, and has one's being in Christ Jesus is a new creation. The old has passed away—that is the Christian's strength and hope.

Yet the Western mainline church struggles with concerns of strength and hope in the twenty-first century. It finds itself in a different kind of wilderness, which has existed only for half a century or so. This wilderness of the church's invisibility for the majority of Western civilization is new. The desire to return to the perceived comfort and safety of the past shows itself in congregational reminiscing and entrenchment, keeping churches self-focused and wandering aimlessly through the desert. Some church leaders know that new life can begin by providing hope that the wilderness is navigable, leading to a promised land. Nonetheless, resistance to intentional wilderness journeying can be fierce. Inviting congregations to live in the tension of the destructive and generative, the letting-go and the co-creating a new thing, often is too frightening for people. As a result, the struggle for mainline denominational survival errs on the side of employing techniques for renewing what is known rather than trusting that something new is evolving. Returning to Egypt to leave the wilderness behind seems preferred to staying in the wilderness for the sake of transformation into a new way of living in faith.

Anxiety about survival is well documented through decades of denominational conversations. Articles citing statistics about declining attendance are met with corresponding programs offering remedies for at-risk and dying congregations. Data permeate conversations about the future of the mainline. Financial and demographic statistics provide churches with information about past, present, and future trends regarding participation.[16] For example, George Hunter indicates:

> The mainline churches of North America are not reaching their receptive neighbors. Although most churches are placed amidst receptive populations, 80 percent of our churches are stagnant or declining. Of the 20 percent growing, 19 out of 20 are growing primarily by transfer and/or biological growth… Less than 1 percent of all the churches in North America grow substantially from conversion growth.[17]

Statistics paint a bleak picture for the church and its work. Evidence of declining attendance constantly reminds church leaders about the competition from megachurches, parachurch organizations,[18] and even other religious movements for participants in mainline congregations. Interpreters of such data often imply that this increasing brokenness in the mainline churches must be fixed quickly with a mighty overhaul of management practices and marketing stances.

Statistics do serve a purpose. Without clear information, hearsay and speculation dominate the conversation about the state of the church. However, statistics can also foster knee-jerk reactions and quick-fix mentalities. The results of such data-sharing practices are clear. Churches often develop anxiety-based mission statements voicing the need to attract young congregants to the church and to teach them the local Christian customs. Oversimplified, quick solutions creep into discussions among members. Denominational anxiety compounds the local church problems by presenting general or regional financial and attendance analyses, followed by insistence on the adoption of formulaic strategies as means for growth and development.[19]

Since the 1960s, denominations and local churches have been calling for leaders who have particular competencies for church development and growth. The struggle to maintain stature in local communities as well as the national public forum has rendered many church leaders reactive, depressed, and burnt-out. Many walk away. For those who have not abandoned the church, the struggle to renew the institution continues, often through church growth programming. The market for church redevelopment and growth materials has grown rapidly in response to the mainline church's decline. An Internet search with the keyword "church growth" yielded 1.7 million options in 2005. In 2007, 7.07 million options are available, an increase of 5.37 million in two years.[20]

Products usually offer formulaic solutions to church decline, if churches follow the scripted program to reach visitors and retain their interest. But tools can provide short-term institutional results without long-term ecclesiological transformation. Churches desiring to pursue quick-fix solutions have a significant set of options. The list of tools is long and ever changing. For example:

> Ever since the 1950s the attempt to seriously address the mystery of mission and the incongruities that arise among mission, strategy, operations and outcomes has led to a variety of organizational change and managerial education ventures—to T-groups (sensitivity training groups), to the whole field called OD (organizational development), to QWL programs (quality of working life), to TQM (total quality management), to Process Re-engineering, and most recently to the use of whole systems interventions such as Real Time Strategic Change, Future Search and Appreciative Inquiry.[21]

If congregations pay little or no attention to changing social contexts, the quick-fixes yield diminished returns within a few years. Nancy Tatom Ammerman, sociology of religion professor at Hartford Seminary, studied twenty-three congregations to determine the relationship between social change and congregational life in the United States. She and her research colleagues sought a sample of places where rapid and significant changes affected congregational communities.[22] To gather data, her team of researchers spoke with demographers, sociologists, religious officials, and journalists. They found that some churches are indeed finding tools that help them think about renewal. Using Appreciative Inquiry[23] as well as hiring leadership coaches exemplifies ways in which congregations gain insights to their relationships and ministries. Leaders in these studies do not rely on the marketplace or the denomination to rescue them, but begin to develop competencies that are particular to their own current theological and social locations. Nonetheless, Ammerman notes that only two established congregations of twenty-three were able to experience rebirth with the aid of a strong minister and support from the denomination.[24]

Useful as particular tools and competencies may be in some instances, they do not provide a process for the ongoing pursuit of the purpose of church, the call to an ever-evolving life of faith that proclaims a message of wholeness and love. These tools, while providing alternative ways to view established organizations and their systems, do not serve to address the foundational call for the church to be the extension of Christ in the world. They promote adaptation to circumstances, perhaps even increase attendance, but do not transform the manner in which individuals live in faith communities, showing love to neighbor and community. Functional change does not address the need for deep, internal change; it simply staves off anxiety for a period of time.

Anxiety has its benefits. Feeling anxious about the future may eventually lead churches to address questions about their identities. Mission statements abound—some simple, some complex—outlining the reasons a church exists. At times, denominations have strongly encouraged local churches to adopt a particular mission statement that focuses on the great commission, going forth and making disciples for Jesus Christ. However, this mission statement, like many tools used for the purpose of "fixing" the church, frequently has remained unexamined by churches and denominations alike. It usually calls the church to pursue persons who will fill the pews and contribute to the offering plate. Growth by conversion is the end-goal. At the same time, the church continues to experience the need to be true to the gospel rather than the world's definition of success-by-numbers fueled by popular interpretations of the commission. The great commandment, to love God and neighbor, often becomes secondary when conversions are a means to power and success.

The phrase "make disciples" is a translation from the Greek verb *mathēteuein*, found in Matthew 28:19. This word is the active verbal form of the noun *mathētēs*, so a more accurate translation is "to disciple." The implication of the verb is to teach, or "teaching how to be disciples." The current appropriation of this biblical text, however, more often than not implies that disciples can be made by human endeavor with some divine participation. Yet human beings *cannot* make disciples, only God can. Nonetheless, an uncritical use of the phrase results in church leaders using this mission focus as a formulaic framework for growing churches rather than as a means of teaching about and pointing toward God's love and desire to be in relationship with all creation.

Indeed, putting the emphasis on this great commission for church growth alone sets struggling congregations on a path of self-destruction. It fosters a sense of scarcity that replaces a focus on abundant blessing. When growth numbers become the primary motivation in the life of a congregation, it is not long before the movement of God has been removed from the conversation. When budgets become the first item on meeting agendas, churches have moved to fear-based existence. This fear perpetuates decline.

The injunction to make disciples as the church's mission therefore, at best, misses the point; it is used as a biblically endorsed commitment to grow the church rather than invite persons to know God's love. At worst, the mission to make disciples becomes coercive in a pluralistic world, spreading a gospel laden with Western values rather than sharing God's love and inviting neighbors into this gift of love. "Making disciples" becomes hollow when wider populations see the church as narrow-minded in its insistence that it is the only institution that offers the one true path to salvation.

Therefore, making disciples as currently understood in many mainline churches differs from sharing that there is good news in the realm of Christianity. Churches that acknowledge the value of pluralism also can be open to learn from other religions or to indigenous understandings of discipleship. Sharing one's narrative on equal terms with another shifts the power differential implied in "making" someone else a disciple. Mutual respect occurs when honest dialogue becomes possible, rather than one party bestowing the right theological and doctrinal answers on an unsuspecting or even hostile audience.[25]

In general, mission statements usually foster a sense of a mission accomplished. The hard work of aligning all ministries to the mission statement often remains ignored, while the relentless search for another method or program to fix the attendance problem continues. Critical reviews of established mission statements rarely occur until a new minister arrives. The cycle of decline continues until churches find themselves incapable of substantial change.[26]

The church ceases to be church when it loses its focus on its ultimate call: to love God, neighbor, and self. When it ceases to be what it is called to be, it not only experiences further decline, but it is in danger of developing into a "lifestyle enclave," a community mirroring the secular world.

> Much of what passes for community in contemporary culture is simply a social extension of individualism. We establish community groups as icons of personal fulfillment, affirmations of consumerism and personal tastes, and bastions of homogeneity.[27]

Robert Wuthnow, sociologist of religion at Princeton University, describes in his research specific groups as communities that become "lifestyle enclaves"; they often exist to support the individual pursuit of healing or social connection. He observes that these groups are gatherings of like-minded persons in primarily uniform demographic settings, practicing a "me-first religion" attitude.[28] The groups form either within the local church or outside of it, because the church does not meet the personal needs of its constituencies. In fact, churches' anxiety about growth, their dispassionate worship, and their inability to care for members adequately are primary reasons for lifestyle enclave development. Thus, churches themselves not only decline, they develop small groups that are inwardly focused rather than attempting to determine the call of the church and its role for the future.

The Question

Underneath the current scramble for the mainline church to grow, or at least reestablish influence and position locally, nationally, and even globally so that it can sustain itself, lurks the deeper question posed earlier: How can the mainline church claim new life based on wholeness and love in a postmodern, globalizing world where many understandings of truth constitute faith? This question presupposes that the mainline is interested in new life for its people and for its neighbors as the most significant reason for its existence.

Claiming new life means refocusing on the great commandment and determining each church's work as a particular response to this mission. Claiming new life also means redefining success as ministry that evokes connection through love in the world. The church's "sacred center," the heart that draws people to it, is anchored in this love.[29]

Success for the church, therefore, would not be ultimately increasing attendance or reestablishing influence, but inviting persons to be transformed through love of God and neighbor, wrapped in a message of hope. Further, rather than claiming success as a secure foundation based on one truth, the mainline church has the opportunity to claim its center as love of God and neighbor, embracing the truths that stem from the great commandment. Only through redefining success by releasing the secular desire for power and influence can the church claim new life. This new life turns on its head the notion that the Western church in particular must decree universal belief systems from within its walls while evangelizing those who are unchurched to adopt the same doctrines and theological viewpoints.

The challenge now is for the church to think differently in the midst of its wilderness. It must invite conversation with the "other" through exploring practices, traditions, yearnings, and creativity that may have been dismissed as irrelevant or even heretical as late as the twentieth century. For example, Jewish traditions and rituals are part of the Christian heritage and can deepen Christian understandings of church history. Buddhist mindfulness speaks to Christian disciplines of centering prayer. The church develops a learning posture rather than a posture of dominance, walking alongside "other" whether such a neighbor is theologically compatible or not.

However, the challenge to connect with neighbors does not assume that the church succumbs to complete relativism or that it must "water down" its faith. There is a grounded focal point for claiming new life, clearly found in the commandment to love God with one's heart, soul, mind, and strength, and to love neighbor as oneself. How churches pursue this commandment will vary. Jesus' statement of the ultimate mission is well defined: the great commandment guides all churches to learn what is required for the process of living into a new life based on wholeness and love.

Nonetheless, much work must be done to engage the question of the mainline church claiming new life in a world of great complexity, alienation, fast change, high anxiety, and a variety of understandings about truth. Thinking differently about the church means learning to look at community in new ways.

It is tempting to relegate mainline history into dichotomies of positive, powerful past and negative, anxious present. Theoretical models and social theories establish contrasts that often are unidirectional and zero-sum, according to sociologist Nancy Ammerman. "More of one meant less than the other. With each step along the way, more of traditional, communal, and religious life is left behind, to be replaced only by modern, rational, world of strangers described in modernization theories."[30]

Yet we know that the unidirectional, linear understanding of the church's evolution does not fit reality. The journey of the church remains much more complex. "Historian Thomas Bender points out that 'if we were to believe every historian who has written about community breakdown in the United States, we would not know whether to place the critical turning point in the 1650s, 1690s, 1740s, 1780s, 1820s, 1850s, 1880s or 1920s.'"[31] Life is more both/and than either/or; thus, the rise of individualism does not preclude more close relationships. It is not that community has disappeared so much as that community lives in the midst of a matrix of communities with complex layers of interactions. Networks of social relations are not defined by an institution itself, including the institution of family, but are social in all kinds of contexts, including the congregation.[32] The complexity of these networks challenges the church to understand itself as part of a larger community rather than as the isolated beacon on a hill. The church is one voice among many in society rather than an authoritative voice listened to by all.

At the congregational level, internal anxiety about the loss of authority and a sense of unique presence in the world constitutes much of the motivation behind the mainline church's desire for change. Attempting to draw new constituencies to the church by introducing contemporary or alternative worship events, a smorgasbord of programming, small group opportunities, and new facilities for family entertainment or sports events exemplify the attempts to rival the myriad activities that are available to people on a daily basis. The church mirrors what seems attractive in society. Because church is one option among many, squeezed into the list of weekly events on individual and family calendars, congregations have reacted by providing more of the same: music that sounds similar to the secular radio station albeit with a different message, programs that entertain while attempting to teach Christian story and principle, and sports or family activities that may not have a theological base other than an opening prayer. Some churches look like entertainment auditoriums or shopping malls. Even many of the mission-focused trips to repair buildings or fund-raisers to provide educational opportunities have counterparts in the secular world or in not-for-profit agencies. So, the church finds itself delivering the Christian message in ways that do not look, feel, or seem much different than the messages of secular society despite a desire to be unique in the world. It has reacted to market pressures to have people "buy in" to its work by appearing secular and therefore familiar.

However, most mainline churches do not have millions of dollars to attract target audiences through advertising as the business world does. They are fighting a losing battle as they try to capture the imaginations of the unchurched or formerly churched through secular mimicry. It is as if the church has lost a sense of what makes it different from the secular world.

> Confronted with a changing environment, congregations seem to draw on the stock of activities they already know and the resources they have at hand more than on any ideological blueprint. Even ideas about the Bible do not necessarily guide a congregation in its decisions about whether to move or stay, whether to change or remain the same. Those decisions are best understood in the matrix of resources and structures that shape the ongoing life of the congregation.[33]

The mainline church, in its own anxiety over its loss of influence in the secularized world, has adopted secular measures to attempt to revitalize itself. By doing so, congregations have lost their emphasis on their own mission, which is to be countercultural: loving God and loving neighbor, the "other," even if the other is a stranger. When churches continue to define success as increasing attendance to remain solvent, or—in cases of large or megachurches—providing training for small churches to grow just as they did, they miss the call to proclaim the good news. Success is being faithful to life-giving connections among friend, stranger, and all creation alike as exemplified by Jesus in the gospels.

Lest the malaise of the mainline be oversimplified as an internal problem, it is necessary to pay attention to contexts in which the churches find themselves. Because the mainline has paid close attention to the consumer culture surrounding it, and, indeed, has in many cases mirrored this culture, it is well aware of the post-9/11, globalizing context in which it exists. Environmental decline, polarized politics, war, mismanaged consumption, and economic brokering all contribute to socioeconomic anxiety that has already become chronic in the twenty-first century. No wonder so many churches adopt quick-fix packages or even close their doors rather than create new frames of reference for the work of the church. Why add more anxiety to an already stressed life? Yet, for those churches and denominations that do wish to change and are struggling to find the path that makes sense and is faithful, there is a process for claiming new life that requires both internal and external work, openness and trust. The first step is to understand the mainline church in its social context both globally and locally, providing perspectives for claiming the new life of wholeness and love, the great hope.

REFLECTION QUESTIONS

1. What are the particularly secular components of congregational life? How do these components play out in worship services or Christian education events? What secular symbols exist in the church building?
2. What would happen if the local church did not focus on church growth and instead focused on deepening its spiritual life? How would job descriptions of staff change? What kinds of groups would be formed? Would preaching change? What kind of studies would be initiated?
3. How does the great commandment play out in terms of the church's location? What would the local church need to change to be more faithful to the great commandment?

3

Church in Global Context

The ancient Greek iconoclast Diogenes, when asked what country he came from, is said to have replied: "I am a citizen of the world."

PETER SINGER[1]

To think about the challenges that the mainline and established evangelical churches face in the early twenty-first century, one must view the broad picture of organized religion and its place in the world. A brief historical survey provides a snapshot of the evolution of the church from its early days as a pluralistic movement, through its establishment as a legal, organized institution—a time called Christendom.

The Evolution of Church

Christianity began as a reform movement within Judaism in rural Palestine. Wandering, charismatic preachers relied on householders for hospitality, while they continued the ministry of Jesus by teaching, healing, and table sharing. These "Jesus theologians," as John Riggs describes them, had little structure to their movement.[2] Titles for Jesus such as "Messiah," contributed to the early emerging church. "Faith that Jesus was God's anointed prophet and king (Messiah) was basic to the definition for the first church."[3] Christian missionaries traveled throughout the Mediterranean basin, attracting attention as they preached about the Messiah. Christianity began organizing itself through house groups and networks. By the end of the first century, Christianity was becoming a significant movement, making an impact in the Greco-Roman world. Further, the pluralistic nature of the movement brought about widespread attention to Christianity as a growing sociopolitical force in the Mediterranean.[4]

By the middle of the second century, conceptual tools and explanations of Christian teachings developed as means to explain theological truths:

> Around the year 200 C.E. the North African thinker Tertullian borrowed from Roman property law to explain ideas about Scripture, Christ, and the Trinity. Principally from Alexandria came the use of Neoplatonism to explain Christian claims. In some ways this was a good conceptual fit because the spiritual realm of Neoplatonic thought, which consisted of a radically other One, an Intellect that contained the organizing principles of reality, and the World Soul, neatly correlated to God, Jesus Christ the Logos of God, and the Spirit.[5]

As the emerging Christian movement developed further in the second through fourth centuries, it produced increasingly uniform standards of doctrine in the midst of diverse cultures and religious traditions, defining itself as it faced challenges from leaders of other religions. Christians, in response, began to form a more coherent identity in the midst of pluralism. "The point for the moment is not that later uniformity was inherently bad but simply that plurality is necessary because Christianity was interpretive from the start."[6]

In 311 Galerius, emperor of Rome, issued an edict of toleration for all religious creeds, thereby legalizing Christianity. In 313 the new emperor, Constantine I, issued the Edict of Milan, which bestowed imperial favor on Christianity for the first time. Constantine himself had a pluralistic mindset, continuing to support pagan deities as well as the Christian God, but is remembered primarily for convening the Council of Nicaea in 325, which contributed to the spread of Christianity even further.[7]

The Nicene Creed established a precedent for councils of bishops located in synods, to create statements of belief and canons of doctrinal authority to unite the church and keep it free from heresy. These theological statements established an orthodoxy, with the intent to define unified beliefs for the Christian world particularly about the nature of Jesus Christ in relation to God. The notion of Christendom, which means "the Christian world," began at this point in history, though the term applies primarily to the fifth through sixteenth centuries, the Middle Ages.[8]

By the early Middle Ages, the church could reinforce obedience to its discipline both in belief and practice through inquisitions and crusades when heresies arose.[9] It also gained significant power through land acquisition and labor. The church had become an important force in Europe. Christendom faced significant challenges, however, by the late Middle Ages, particularly at the advent of the Protestant Reformation:

> The disintegration of Christendom began at the close of the Middle Ages with the rise of nationalism, the Reformation and the inevitable secularization of society which followed the Renaissance. The Reformers themselves hardly foresaw the break-up of Christendom which was to come, for even in the Protestant countries the reception of the sacraments was still enforced by the magistrates, and heresy and even dissent were offences against the state.[10]

The ideal of church-state partnership did not survive the quest for human freedom of religion and political rule. People challenged church power, at times violently, as an instrument of aristocratic rule:

> The forces overthrowing the hegemony of Christian religion in Europe and its satellites can be traced as far back as the breakdown of the medieval synthesis of faith and reason. But more conspicuously, they made themselves felt in the Enlightenment of the eighteenth century and are punctuated politically by the French and (in some respects) the American revolutions.[11]

In the late sixteenth and seventeenth centuries, Protestant Christianity provided the Western European church with detailed doctrinal systems, based on a theory of scripture that had not been held by classical Reformers themselves. Biblical infallibility, the verbal words of God spoken and recorded verbatim, led to literalism with accompanying doctrinal and organizational structures of power. In response, Pietism emerged in the last third of the seventeenth century, focusing on the experiential nature of religion, the religion of the heart. Pietists organized themselves in small groups for scripture study, peacefully accepted other Christians and focused on ministerial skill in pastoral arts.[12]

The evolution of the church in post-Christendom rendered it less powerful in each progressing century. In the late eighteenth century, the French Revolution and the establishment of independent states in North America brought about the secular state, dividing church from state so that the church no longer controlled civil society. The ideals of democracy, citizenship, and inalienable rights rose to the fore at this time.

In the late nineteenth century, "modern theology" reexamined orthodox theology in light of the need for the church to "come to terms with scientific, critical and historical developments in the post-Enlightenment world."[13] Modernists differed sharply among themselves, but shared a philosophy of truth as essentially contextual, addressing themselves to the historical development of Christianity. They understood the church to be a necessary historical extension of the gospel.[14]

In the early 1900s, modern theology had begun to devolve into Western cultural religion. "God was the kindly Father. Jesus was the moral example that showed us by his life what our hearts really knew. And under the guidance of such a God and Savior the West was making progress as Christianity helped bring civilization to the world."[15]

The imperialist nature of Christianity, often hidden in the notion of evangelism, posed a danger for the world as it attached Western cultural values to itself. As European and North American societies gained strength, the good news of the gospel became embedded in the good news of Western, capitalist culture:

> [D]uring the Christendom and modern eras there was a frequently uncritical and sometimes tragic identification of Western culture with Christianity. The two marched arm-in-arm into non-Western cultures and lands, suggesting by their

close alliance that to embrace Western culture and its norms was to embrace Christianity, and vice versa. Of course, in a time when in the U.S. being a good Christian was not particularly different from being a responsible citizen, it would make sense that as Christianity encountered other cultures and faiths around the world, Western culture and values were all wrapped up with the Christian faith.[16]

As mainline Christianity continued to be shaped by Western culture, it began to lose its distinctive voice in society. Indeed, it is not news to anyone that today the church is less influential in Western societies than it was in the first half of the twentieth century, despite its carrying Western cultural norms throughout the world. This waning influence not only illustrates the death of Christendom beginning centuries ago, it brings into question the vitality and role of the church in the Western world altogether in this age.

Post-Christendom and Anti-Secularism

How can the mainline church claim new life based on wholeness and love in a postmodern, globalizing world where many truths constitute faith? Revisiting the question before the church establishes the focus for inquiry required for gaining a wider perspective of the context in which the church finds itself. Theologian Douglas John Hall discusses the contrast between the church of Christendom and the post-Christendom institutions of today.[17] Christendom throughout the Middle Ages allowed Christian clergy to associate closely with civic leaders, powerful organizations, and government entities: the power establishments. The church's presence was an unquestioned part of these establishments. Further, the Christian religion identified itself with dominant races and classes. A significant component of living in the Christendom era was that the good news of the gospel was not necessarily life-changing news; it was not appealing as a countercultural alternative to power establishments, but rather a sanctioned, law-abiding way of living.

Hall claims that Christianity in the Western world no longer has a seat at the table of political, social, and economic establishments, but is slow to realize the implications of this disenfranchisement.[18] Indeed, though the decline of Christendom has been occurring for centuries, it has become most noticeable in the twentieth century. Author Wayne Schwab states "[I]f there is any truism today, it is that the institutional church at every level of its life is fairly well excluded from participating in the decisions that shape life in today's world."[19] Many mainline churches still believe that the church should have influence on secular establishments and that Christian behavior and practice should remain the norm for law-abiding, pious citizens. In fact, the opposite is true. The church has adopted societal norms such as modeling business practices in hopes of regaining influence in public life. Instead, by adopting the secular norms, churches have reversed the path of influence, allowing post-Christendom society to dictate behaviors and practices to the church.

Yet, living on the margins of Western society, even unintentionally, can yield a necessary inquiry about the nature and mission of the mainline church. "One of the opportunities and necessities of our new age is to unwrap the package and for Western Christians to become as discerning about their own culture and its biases as they are about any other."[20]

Hall calls the church to exercise its best work at the margins of society. He writes, "From the edges, from the sidelines, it is possible for the once-mainline church to exercise a prophetic ministry, a public witness that it could not easily bring off and seldom did bring off when it was still an unquestioned part of the Establishment."[21] The good news of the gospel is best heard and understood where privilege and power do not rule. Love of neighbor makes the most impact when advocacy and care for those already existing on the margins are the focus of the church's work. However, Hall needs to delve deeper into a global Christian context, paying attention to a reactive backlash against secularism, before this vision for the church can be realized.

Despite the death of Christendom and the rise of Western secularism, Christian movements are growing in the global South and East.[22] While Western mainline churches experience decline, Christianity, Islam, and indigenous religions increase their influence on the peoples of many countries in Latin America, Africa, and Asia. Different religious traditions in countries at different stages of economic development are beginning to critique the Western emphasis on secular advancement for personal and national gain. Scott

Thomas, in his article "The Global Resurgence of Religion," indicates that this resurgence exposes a crisis of modernity, namely reflecting a deep disillusionment with perspectives that "reduce the world to that which can be perceived and controlled through reason, science, technology and bureaucratic rationality, and leaves out considerations for the spiritual or sacred dimensions of life."[23] Fundamentalist religious movements throughout the world, including Christianity, show strong, sometimes violent rejection of modern secularism:

> These studies [on fundamentalism] found considerable simi-
> larities in these movements of conservative religion. Among
> these similarities is a strong rejection of modern secularism,
> although not modern technology (which is often used effec-
> tively to get across their message). All of these movements
> seek to reinstate a union of religion and state, making strict
> religious observance of one dominant state religion the law
> of the land. In other words, they seek a Hindu, Buddhist,
> Christian, Jewish or Islamic state, rejecting the modern
> development of separation of "church" and state. Religious
> pluralism, differences of religious worldview, both within
> the established religion and outside it, the tolerance of many
> religious traditions in the same society, all are rejected.[24]

Particularly in the Western world, Christian fundamentalism advocates even more strongly than the mainline church for Christendom's recovery, with proponents accusing the mainline and evangelical churches themselves for capitulating to secular society rather than having insisted on a normative behavioral ethic and personal piety designed to usher in the realm of God on earth.[25] This critique of the mainline church's capitulation may contain seeds of truth. Nonetheless, the fundamentalist voice in the Western world, while publicly ubiquitous in the early twenty-first century, does not receive much credence from the majority of Western populations. Therefore, Christian fundamentalism has not been and is unlikely to be successful in reinstating Christendom in the West.

In the global South and East, Christian movements may be growing, but they are not primary influencers at the table of economic and political powers, at least not yet. Instead, Christianity is a faith that motivates grassroots development and liberation movements in "Two-Thirds World" countries. Christianity calls them to raise their voices for human rights and dignity in protest against economic and political powers rather than as a means to become the powers themselves. These movements create indigenous theologies, locating the gospel in specific microcultures and providing hope in particular contexts. Thus, Christendom, the Christian world that has power over or within secular establishments, is not prevalent in these countries either. Ultimately, Christendom has not been reestablished in the current age despite efforts to do so.

Globalization

Understanding the death of Christendom provides one context for the mainline church's self-awareness. The rise of global connections among cultures and faith practices adds another layer of complexity for the church to consider. "Globalization" may be defined as the compression of the world, referring both to increasing sociocultural interdependence and to rapidly expanding political and cultural consciousness. Globalization is simultaneously cultural, economic, and political, but not necessarily cohesive normatively; instead, it is networked multidimensionally in a complex and constantly changing web.[26]

Globalization, it can be argued, has existed since explorers set out to discover new worlds, bringing their own cultures to bear in the midst of existing religious and social constructs. What has emerged as unique in the twentieth century, with roots in the eighteenth and nineteenth centuries, is the primary focus on success defined as globally based economic gain. The rise of secularism and the de-divinization of nature contributed to this shift:

> If we compare our civilization with pre-modern cultures, the difference between growth and equilibrium springs to mind. Those pre-modern civilizations were anything but "primitive" or "underdeveloped." On the contrary, they were highly complicated systems of equilibrium which ordered the relation of people to nature and the gods. It is only modern Western civilizations that for the first time are one-sided, programmed solely toward development, growth, expansion and conquest.[27]

Globalization is often discussed with little reference to religion and faith practice; politics and economics laced with an implicit set of ethics tend to be the focus.[28] Little place is given to the church in the global conversation, though the mainline church must itself focus on global connections as it co-creates its future with God. Without attention to the world's peoples and their struggles, the church cannot live with integrity into its mission to love God and neighbor. Globalization has economic consequences for all countries; a globalizing world opens connections with anyone in any country, so the definitions of "neighbor" have expanded exponentially within the span of the twentieth and early twenty-first centuries. These impacts of globalization on local communities provide significant challenges for the church.

While Western nations experience dislocation in terms of political power and economics, and at the same time make efforts to define clearly their geographic boundaries or location, human beings are affected in two ways. First, job loss spreads to all economic echelons as companies downsize or outsource work to cheaper labor forces. Competition that both initiates and responds to consumerism falls apart when local economies cannot support themselves:

> The breaking of the old social contract is the result of three fundamental forces. The global economy simultaneously permits, encourages, and forces companies to move their activities to the lowest-cost locations. Since the moving costs are large, it usually pays companies to attempt to force down costs in their current locations to derive benefits of lower wages without having to pay moving costs.[29]

Second, global communication creates instant access to international conversation and idea-sharing from homes even in the most rural areas of Western nations. A result of armchair communication is the privatization of ethics without benefit of local community input.

Christianity does not enter the global conversation because faith seems to have little to do with economics or communication other than when used to justify one's own ethics and subsequent behavior. Bypassing religious conversation is easier than it ever has been before. Mary McClintock Fulkerson, a professor of theology, describes the phenomenon this way:

As these accounts (globalization theories) explain it, new forms of global capitalist technology create common "cultures" with no sense of place or memory. The commodification that is inherent to capitalism opens cultural meaning to a process of universalization, where meanings that are shared by particular communities get detached from those specific locales and their histories. In addition to the abstracting of meaning from its specific context, profit-motivated media "clean it up" as well. Thus meaning is divested not only of locale, but of finitude, complexity and ambiguity.[30]

Many church leaders continue to strive for a place in the economic and ethics conversation, often by becoming political figures or creating organizations that vie for media attention. These leaders hope to make an impact on lawmakers or corporate decision-makers as well as the general public while they create names for themselves. The danger arises when the media portray Christian leaders in ways that suit media corporations:

> We can better understand these negative consequences of religious use of the media if we consider the dominant styles within the media and their impact on habits of reception and engagement. Shifts in media influence the relationships between senders and receivers. Insofar as religious leaders disseminate their message and attempt to maintain their authority through the infrastructures of contemporary media, their message will be recoded and received by their audience in a manner consistent with those media. In the present context of corporate culture industries, this brings a series of problems associated with particular class interest and practices of the new cultural intermediaries.[31]

Too often, these church leaders have attempted to stay at the table by adopting cultural norms established by the consumer-based industry, developing power networks, and engaging the rules of politics as one of the would-be important players.

Counter-establishment voices[32] do exist. They strive to change political policies and business decision-making by refocusing churches and synagogues on social issues such as poverty and health care. They often face a divided group of religious leaders as they notice colleagues becoming part of the establishment in question. However, in this international media age, even a counter-establishment church remains in danger of becoming one more local or global agency providing public statements and human services where they are perceived to be needed. Further, the mainline church reacts to moral issues as they arise in public life, rather than claiming its own voice by initiating movements for the dignity of humanity and the wholeness of human life:

> In the era of nation-states the international character of the church was one of its most significant features, just to the extent the church offered an alternative to the loyalties bred through nationalism. Though the church often failed to challenge nationalism, its very existence at least provided the material possibility for mounting a challenge to the state's pretension to rule over minds and bodies. Yet, Boyle suggests, in the new global order, the church's universality may be an even more serious temptation than the temptation to nationalism since the Reformation. For the new order is a kind of universality whose ambition is to rule minds and bodies just as nations did so effectively in the past. The church may be tempted to collaborate with these worldly powers, celebrating the fact that they have adopted the church's global perspective.[33]

Worldly powers have their own purposes, often defining human beings as rational subjects who pursue their own self-interest, mostly through economic possessions. People are consumers. Economic wealth is equated with human well-being, and, hence, with happiness. Rosemary Radford Ruether states this mindset well: "The more one owns, the better off one is. The better off one is, the happier one will be."[34] Possessions are equated with consumption and domination of nature with the assumption that limitless growth in terms of resources and economics is possible. Little attention is given to distribution of goods, to power differentials between transnational corporations and local workers, or to human dignity. The market system is considered inevitable because it has been defined as the means of human progress.[35]

Consumer culture presents another new (but likewise not unprecedented) problem for theology and the church. Our analysis has shown that the danger of cultural erosion in globalizing capitalism is not something faced only by fragile, dominated cultures; it also endangers the Western traditions at the heart of the societies that have originated and profit from globalization. Thus, many of the concerns of theologies of mission and inculturation are now relevant to first-world cultures.[36]

One only has to notice the messages found in advertising to realize that those who matter are those with spending power. Television and Internet commercials indicate that everything is available for a price. The global economy also confronts people with a global social economy. Travelers note in cities throughout the world the presence of shopping areas with the same stores and same fast-food chains. The homeless, either displaced persons who cannot afford housing and live with friends or people living on the streets, are part of life even in small towns. Bank and mortgage companies change frequently, communication companies merge quickly, energy corporations become conglomerates, and jobs are outsourced; in short, people have become commodities themselves, implying disposability along with the rest of creation.[37]

Globalization also has its benefits as well as its challenges. Scientific and technological discoveries have contributed to breakthroughs in science and medicine. Development of advanced communication and transportation technologies has fostered greater awareness of social and cultural diversity with the opportunity for greater networking than ever before.

The advent of massively available communication means that the opportunities for learning will be greater than ever. A child in a remote, rural village in India can receive instruction from a great thinker who is thousands of miles away. A doctor who is preparing for a rare operation can watch a narrated video of the same operation that was conducted by the world's authority in that specialization. A researcher in bioengineering will have efficient access to all the information that has ever been recorded in the field. The potential for "global connectedness" means that we will have the opportunity to interact in a way that leads to the rapid and positive evolution of our species.[38]

The complexity of embracing benefits that serve the majority of populations while challenging ethics that benefit only those in power remains the struggle for this century. For example, Peter Singer describes this complexity by naming how interdependence and global accountability to local people preclude independent action by any nation state:

> When different nations led more separate lives, it was more understandable—though still quite wrong—for those in one country to think of themselves as owing no obligations, beyond that of non-interference, to people in another state. But those times are long gone. Today, as we have seen, our greenhouse gas emissions alter the climate under which everyone in the world lives. Our purchases of oil, diamonds, and timber make it possible for dictators to buy more weapons and strengthen their hold on the countries they tyrannize. Instant communications show us how others live, and they in turn learn about us and aspire to our way of life. Modern transport can move even relatively poor people thousands of miles, and when people are desperate to improve their situation, national boundaries prove permeable.[39]

Ultimately, trends in the globalizing world bring challenges of balancing complex impacts, both negative and positive, on local communities. For example, mass-produced products such as clothing or music sold throughout the world result in conformity of style and also lower prices for those unable to afford custom-made items. Local communities connect to communities on the other side of the planet and also become physically isolated as jobs move to more lucrative markets, leaving behind a devastated local economy. Cultural experiences of one country teach others about diversity and also establish pressure to adopt particular cultural norms to acquire what is perceived as a successful, happy life. Research teams benefit from global sharing of medical breakthroughs and also do not contextualize results to particular populations and social locations. Daily newscasts indicate that all of these factors are at play in the world today.

As the mainline church acknowledges this global meta-context with its propensity to draw the world together through technology and communication while harming local markets, denominations as well as local congregations find themselves in a position to make a choice: they can continue to strive to have a voice that works in conjunction with socioeconomic powers such as governments and transnational corporations, or they can turn to prophetic work on the margins of society, as Hall suggested earlier. If the church chooses the latter, it will find freedom to critique the negative aspects of globalization in light of a Christian ethic: loving God and neighbor, respecting creation and promoting human dignity and wholeness over and against marketplace profit margins. The potential for the church, and indeed, other religions, to influence secular powers from this ethical point of view remains significant. Those who engage in a proactive, change-oriented task of ethical living and discourse promote a new kind of influence based on love of neighbor: wholeness, justice, and hospitality for each and for all peoples.

In addition to living in post-Christendom and globalized contexts, the church faces the trends of what is known as "postmodernity." Postmodernism in conjunction with the other movements afoot in the world has the greatest potential effect on the mainline church's self-understanding and ability to bring the message of hope to a hurting world. Attention to values and characteristics of postmodern peoples adds to the complexity of the world in which the church finds itself in the current era.

REFLECTION QUESTIONS

1. How does globalization affect the local church? How does the local church affect the world?
2. What unique message does the church bring to the world? What does that message mean for ministry in the local church?
3. How can churches participate in minimizing the negative impacts of globalization for themselves and for other communities? What kind of voice does the local church desire to have in the midst of secular organizations and corporations? How will it make its voice heard?

4

Church in Postmodern Context

Postmodernity promises neither clarification nor the disappearance of perplexity.

GRAHAM WARD[1]

While the mainline church currently wanders in the wilderness, individuals continue their search for meaningful existence. One of the ways persons do so is by defining what they are against in social, religious, and political arenas. For example, voters may not know what they define as their own platform for change, but they know when they do not like the sound of someone else's platform. They are just as likely to vote against a candidate as they are for one.

This particular approach toward finding meaning introduces a new problem for mainline and established churches. In the twentieth and twenty-first centuries, most Western civilizations reject institutionalized Christianity, claiming the church to be irrelevant and out-of-date. Three responses emerge. One has been to abandon interest in Christian community altogether. Another has been to remain connected to the church through small groups, but to challenge its traditional theological and doctrinal stances.[2] A third has resulted in leaders developing loosely organized faith movements or house groups (emerging churches), that are not denominationally based or church-connected and that do not subscribe to particular theological schools of thought.

43

Persons who know what they stand against in terms of institutionalized church teaching and behavior still experiment to determine what they stand for in their own belief systems. People who show Christian sympathies but claim no allegiance to the institutionalized church often attempt to create their own privatized belief systems, invented or compiled from more than one religious tradition or from a variety of theological viewpoints in Christianity itself. This *bricolage,* a synthesis of ideas or practices that happen to be available, contributes little to religious tradition because there is little inquiry into intent of ideas and practices.[3] It also allows for creative preservation of ancient traditions as found in Latino popular religion, engaging the ancient cultural systems in new ways.[4] For example, people often develop faith practices that include a variety of meditations, rituals, prayers, and experiences that suit personal tastes and needs.

Many of those remaining in the church find themselves questioning issues of biblical authority despite their churches' teachings. As a result, they are searching for historical context and literary nuance in the sacred texts. At the same time, many Christians do believe the truth claims offered by doctrinal law or theological orthodoxy. Theological and doctrinal tensions and paradoxes contribute to both evangelical and progressive Christians examining their own faith constructs in small groups, sometimes mixing together for lively discussion.

Another segment of the self-declared Christian population initiates its own gatherings for conversation and worship based on niche contexts.[5] These groups usually arise when leaders in churches become disillusioned with their own institutions. They privilege spiritual experience through conversation, sensual settings, and music.[6] This segment of Christians is popularly known as the emerging church movement. It understands itself to be creating its own ecclesiology, its own way of "being church." Because this movement echoes some of the emerging movements in history that critiqued the established church and also uses sophisticated media and communication, it has what appears to be a relevant, though perhaps transitional impact on the quest for meaning prevalent in the public domain. Discussion of emerging churches follows later in this chapter.

The search for meaning in any of these venues adds a complex layer to the previously discussed post-Christendom status of the mainline church. Privatized faith and abandonment of long-established institutions in favor of contemporary practices and sites further minimize the potential of the church to provide a unique message of good news for the age. At the same time, the desire for spiritual development is accompanied by a growing awareness of global conversation influencing personal belief systems. Each of the three arenas named resulting from the rejection of the current institutionalized state of the church, namely the quest for spirituality outside the church, the quest for deeper meaning within the church, and the quest for a new way of being church altogether, share a variety of characteristics that have been dubbed "postmodern."

Postmodernism

The historian Arnold Toynbee coined the term *postmodern* in the 1940s in response to the modern era.[7] "Postmodernism," however, has not been categorically defined, arguably because of the descriptors used for the term itself: acceptance of plurality while rejecting the grand narratives (or meta-narratives) that describe progress and truth, consumerism on a global scale, personal experience as primary authority, and fads driven by symbols.[8] Theologian Peter Hodgson describes this plurality by indicating that African American faith in the United States, liberation theologies in developing countries, and European political theology have all set forth a challenge to a white Western, monolithic understanding of the church. Postmodern movements are pluralistic, emancipatory, prophetic, and transformative, challenging patriarchy. Postmodern thinking leads to ecumenical and interreligious dialogues, reminding the church that Christianity is a global religion, needing to enter into genuine, potentially transformative dialogue with other faiths.[9] Proponents of postmodern thinking do not conform to particular generational categories, socioeconomic strata, or racial-ethnic demographics.

Postmodern thinking attempts to interconnect reason, ancient tradition, experience, and revelation. While postmoderns argue against an absolute truth, a meta-narrative that is true for everyone, thinkers in this age indicate that there exists some foundational truth, but it is embedded in context. Therefore, convictions about the nature of reality remain relative to perspective. In other words, descriptions of truth that attempt to be decontextualized are problematic because they are incapable of being context-free; therefore, there can be no universal truth claim. Even if theologians, scientists, or philosophers claim a universal truth through logical analysis, they themselves cannot claim to be context- or influence-free; their own ethics and values inform their avenues of inquiry. There is no such thing as objective observation for postmoderns. If institutions such as the church claim truth, they are regarded with skepticism, if not suspicion for the same reason.

Continued attempts to define postmodernism lead to defining what it is not. Postmodernism differs from modernism though it is not its opposite. Modernity, credited in origin to the figures of the Enlightenment era (seventeenth and eighteenth centuries), advocated for reason as the means of establishing an authoritative system of ethics, logic, and governmental organization, as well as a mechanism by which philosophers could obtain objective truth about the universe. Inspired by Newtonian physics, Enlightenment thinkers argued that the same kind of systematic thinking could apply to all forms of human activity. Reason, science, rationality, and empirical study all applied to the working of society and the state. These thinkers believed that progress depended on removal of superstition, irrational thought, and authority based on emotional experience.[10]

The Enlightenment informed modernity's influence on theology, resulting in an emphasis on reason and dislocating God to a distant transcendence with little or nothing to do with the daily affairs of humanity.[11] "For interconnected with all the characteristics of modernity is its secularism, achieved by the banishment of God from the world, at first into a 'heaven' to which one might aspire after death, and eventually out of consideration altogether for practical and public purposes."[12] Further, by its nature modernity valued itself as a state of thinking that, at a fundamental level, should not rely on revelation or subjectivity. As a result, modernity established clear-cut dichotomies naming distinct categories for right/wrong, insider/outsider, rational/emotional, and good/evil. Those who did not fit the definition of "right, rational, and good" (the insider), were at best, not taken seriously, or, at worst, defamed (the outsider).

Modernity, with these characteristics notwithstanding, is as difficult to define as postmodernity. References to the "modern period" are philosophically, but not temporally, related to the Enlightenment period in the seventeenth and eighteenth centuries, where the rational, stable, objective, knowable self was a product of rational science producing universal, eternal truths about the world. A commonly held notion at this time was the inevitability of progress toward an ultimate end. However, modernity as a time frame arrives later, after eighteenth century Romanticism[13] and the nineteenth century Victorian period.[14] The modern period encompasses the late nineteenth century through the Second World War (1890s–1945). Revolutionary political movements such as fascism, Nazism, communism, and anarchism stated their visions for a great future during this time. Modernists reacted against the Victorian period where capitalism, decorum, belief in the empire, and domesticity were of primary value. It was in this period that explorations of subjectivity and alternative thinking about the meaning of life began. Poets and artists in this time period introduced cubism (an attempt to see the same object from different perspectives simultaneously) and experimental writing.

Postmodernism can be understood either as a reaction "against" modernism or a natural evolution of modernism with correctives to its assumptions surfacing through time. In fact, one school of postmodern thought describes postmodernism as a constructive commitment to the unfinished character of modernity, devoted to human dignity and justice. This postmodernism takes seriously reason and experience as means of knowing emerging truths.[15]

> Postmodernism is a term used in a variety of contexts to describe social conditions, movements in the arts, economic and social conditions and scholarship from the perspective that there is a definable and differentiable period after the modern, or that the 20th century can be divided into two broad periods. It is an idea that has been extremely controversial and difficult to define among scholars, intellectuals and historians because the term implies to many that the modern historical period has passed.[16]

It would be a stretch to think that postmodernism will solve the ills of modernity. The dichotomies introduced as categories of rational thought have divided strangers, communities, and nations; much work will need to be done to reestablish healthy relationships and a sense of wholeness in the world. "Across chasms of noncommunication, what bridges can be built? The first pilings in such a bridge may have to be sheer hope that the bridge is possible. Tutu's word is the right one: 'moral-religious hope rather than empirical-rational optimism based on "the facts.""""[17]

Postmodernism faces challenges beyond healing the divisions developed in modern times. The greatest criticism of postmodernism is that postmoderns have no foundational narrative or truth upon which to build their meaning. In other words, extreme relativity can lead to privatized faith or even powerlessness to find meaning beyond the self. Lois Schawver, instructor at the School of Professional Psychotherapy in California, attempts to answer this criticism by speaking of a "visionary postmodernism," an evolution of new dreams after a period of disillusionment. For Schawver, postmodernism is a natural step forward from modernism, creating opportunity to correct the mistakes of the past.[18]

New dreams include lessons from tradition, but also provoke rejection of what has betrayed prior generations, while invoking new hopes for the future. The pursuit of truth, or truths, begins to find new avenues of inquiry, rejecting dichotomous categories and universal truths.

> Since the human ability to know truth is finite, postmodern thinkers tend to be wary of any person or institution that offers or demands a universal and infinite view, suspecting such perspectives are often rooted in a desire to control, manipulate, or even do violence to others.
>
> Postmodernism also explains some of the impulses of this emerging culture. Emerging culture persons prefer spiritual worldviews to the mechanistic and scientific explanations of the previous age's modernism.[19]

Because of new avenues of inquiry and openness to experience as informative, postmoderns tend to value creativity and playfulness, expressing themselves through pop-culture and current technology and media. Experimentation and ambiguity characterize postmodern expression. Transparency is an important characteristic for postmoderns. For example, architecture itself in the postmodern era prizes transparency; it keeps internal structures such as air ducts, supports, and building materials visible to the observer.[20]

Postmodernism in the West and the Emerging Church

Postmoderns desire to know the world through indigenous narratives and corresponding traditions. To them, God is both transcendent and immanent, separate from but active in human life. If they choose to attend a faith community, they will look for a transcendent experience of God in the midst of intimate surroundings. This experience occurs when holy space (*temenos*) and time (*kairos*) are created in worship experiences so that the senses are engaged as fully as possible while only simple, usually ancient, liturgies or meditations are spoken. Silence during worship speaks loudly to these participants. Postmoderns distrust long, wordy liturgies that are supposed to convey meaning and reject a cerebral theology that does not touch the whole person. Instead, they are recovering a mystical and liturgical spirituality as they imagine could have been found in the early church. Postmoderns dislike megachurches, which are often auditorium-like spaces, depersonalized and performance-oriented.[21]

Postmodern faith challenges decontextualized, dogmatic expressions of universal truth and embraces the desire to keep hope alive amidst struggle, angst, and "lostness" in the midst of community. Thus, narratives of hope and transformation are important aspects of faith and theology.[22] Indeed, postmoderns desire to build their own narratives of hope and wholeness. They will challenge faith communities to which they relate to "give back" to the world. If faith claims and practices are not matched with meaningful works in the world, then postmoderns soon lose interest in their worshiping community. Therefore, the focus on manifesting the great commandment in daily living makes sense to them. To love neighbor means to pray and to work toward wholeness and justice for humanity and creation.

Postmodern thinking and experience strive to develop a spirituality of connectedness that rejects modernism's dichotomous emphases, basing faith on what Mary Grey calls "the theme of the prophetic heart." She describes the prophetic heart as "soulscape" because it integrates "interiority with external political and social circumstances into a contemplative faith responsive, in freedom, to the vulnerability of God."[23] Grey's soulscape addresses the postmodern desire to experience God's internal movement personally and communally, resulting in response to external contexts. This internal and external experience-action shapes life meaning for postmoderns.

Postmodern persons, if they cannot find a worship space that satisfies their desire for transcendent experience, will create their own *temenos* and *kairos*. They do not hesitate to gather peers in order to create a worship atmosphere that conveys depth of discourse and meaningful experience. Formal organizational structures and professional clergy represent institutional religion to postmoderns, something they either try to change or avoid.

Theologically, Christian postmoderns who invite discourse about God's nature and search for experience of God's presence expect a God who lives up to the teachings and works Jesus exemplified in the gospels. Theology consistent with faithful practice indicates authenticity. For instance, to a Western postmodern person the theological claim that God predestined Jesus, a beloved son, to be killed by torturous means to prove a point for the greater good or to provide salvation sounds false when God is also upheld as a loving God. The loving God commands human beings to love one another, tend to each other, and challenge unjust institutions that hurt creation. Ambiguity about the complex nature of God is acceptable in postmodern circles, but perceived direct contradictions in theological teaching from the church pose significant difficulties for those who do not think in absolutes or polarities.

The "emerging church" movement is one response to the postmodern desire for noninstitutional, experiential and relational faith. This movement epitomizes postmodern gatherings because each community creates its own niche depending on its participants' needs and tastes. Each community looks different, but all eschew traditional institutional organization and worship. In fact, emerging church Christians spend more time talking about faith in secular environments than sacred ones. Conversations at pubs, coffee houses, sports events, or on the Internet all are considered legitimate ways of "being church."

Emerging churches are capturing attention particularly in Europe, Australia, New Zealand, Canada, and the United States. They are part of a trend that shows that people are moving away from a consumer economy to an "experience economy." People are searching for experiences rather than mere products or passive entertainment. Consumers are bored.

> They go to the same old shopping malls, see the same old shops, view the same old brands and they long for something new, something exciting, something that will arrest their attention.
>
> This has created an appetite for experiences, which retailers and manufacturers are hurrying to meet. Many restaurants, for example, see their prime activity as providing a particular experience of eating, rather than just selling food.[24]

Further, people are searching for life-transforming experiences. Postmodern Christians or explorers who gravitate toward communities that offer opportunity for transformation find the emerging church movement a likely venue for such an experience.

"Emerging" movements constitute a broad category of churches; they are reinventing themselves in terms of worship and mission geared to postmoderns. Leaders are starting new life communities that bear little resemblance to traditional understandings of church. However, categorizing this movement proves difficult. Indeed, emerging church leaders often do not wish to be categorized; they simply see themselves as entrepreneurs creating a new way of being church. Eddie Gibbs and Ryan Bolger spent five years researching emerging communities through observation, interviews with fifty leaders, document analysis, and personal experience:

> This study of emerging churches represents a determined attempt to identify the key practices of this disparate movement, which is so diverse and fragmented that some observers and insiders do not like to think of it as a movement at all. For insiders, it is more of a conversation. The challenge is to identify these communities and to clarify the concerns that motivate these ground-level leaders to reshape and redirect the church in all aspects of its life. Although the communities they lead may be small in number, the numbers are growing rapidly as their influence spreads through websites, blogs, chat rooms, and conference interactions.[25]

The "Emergent" church, a sub-group of the "emerging church" movement, was founded by a particular group of evangelical leaders who have a large Web-based network of constituents throughout the world.[26] Emergent churches attempt to embrace postmodern sensibilities and turn their attention to the marginalized at the same time. It remains to be seen whether these self-defined new movements understand themselves as embracing a post-Christendom, alternative faith community mind-set or whether they are beginning to exhibit denominational qualities, albeit on the Internet and through regular national gatherings. There is some danger of developing community enclaves in the Emergent church based on heavy reliance on its leadership. Nonetheless, many of these churches and online communities focus outside themselves, combating worldwide poverty as a primary social justice mission while also giving energy to evangelizing unchurched young and middle-aged populations.

Whether connected to the particular Emergent network or simply creating new space and ways to be in community, emerging churches focus on experiential worship and ongoing conversation about faith's impact on daily life. These churches or house groups show great technological skill and use media effectively; they do not attempt to "blend" twentieth-century contemporary and traditional worship so much as create a setting with multiple visual and aural stimuli designed for high levels of participation. In emerging churches the postmodern propensity to multitask plays out in worship services. For example, in some churches, one can be singing, working on an art project, and pause to receive communion within the space of five minutes. Other emerging churches invite affinity groups to form small faith communities: for example, bikers, professors, gangs, college study groups, Goths, or teens. They too face the danger of becoming community enclaves, though often experience significant turnover so do not necessarily become closed groups.

The idea for emerging churches is to appropriate faith in ways that connect with ancient tradition and at the same time provide a contemporary experience, recreating traditions to make them meaningful in current context. The creative aspect of worship not only allows self-expression but also provides a means for communities to participate in the creative nature of God.[27] Worship awakens a sense that participants' lives matter; they are grounded in a rich history and also feel an urgency to "make a difference in the world" for the sake of future generations. This "ancient-new" approach to church appeals more to postmoderns than what has been deemed "contemporary worship." Emphasis on creativity as an expression of God's gift to human beings keeps worship dynamic and ever-relevant to the cultures from which participants come. Emerging church leaders know that top-down control of static worship will not hold the attention of postmodern groups of any age or demographic.

In many emerging churches, encouraging creative expression involves taking risks in worship, with emphasis on experimentation. What occurs in the worship space and time is indigenous to that particular gathering. Use of denominational or recently published, mass-produced resources for music and prayer seems inauthentic to participants. Leaders themselves facilitate what happens on any given worship day without prescribing the style of worship that will occur. Attendees prefer to create their own worship in a space they design themselves. The result is a sense of organized chaos at every gathering, complete with elements of surprise throughout worship or conversation time together. In the midst of this chaos, playfulness and humor add to the sense of worshiping as an authentic community. Participants are less concerned with relevance or theological stances than they are with authentic experience in community.[28]

Though it sounds like a contradiction, emphasis on creativity does not preclude use of ancient traditions and liturgies. While recently published worship resources are not attractive to participants in emerging churches, the ancient practices are:

> We want to be involved creatively in the processes rather than become consumers of someone else's creative efforts... creativity should not always be the process of creating new things. We are living in a post-novelty world. Things are not more valuable if they are newly created. Creativity in the sense of inventing new forms (how traditional church views it) can be a negative thing. There is a surplus of invention and resources.[29]

Thus, emerging churches prefer to retrieve ancient practices such as Gregorian chant or creedal recitation rather than invent new ones. These practices are to be rediscovered and then experienced in the present context; thus creativity meets the ancient and makes it new again. Completely new forms or practices of worship are believed simply to add to a plethora of practices already available and therefore do not serve any significant purpose.

Four challenges result from spontaneous creativity. First, sustainability of a worshiping community can be difficult when spontaneity is valued. The facilitator has a role to play as organizer, calling people together at given times. Consistency of attendance is less important in terms of sustainability than venue availability at published times so that anyone who wishes to participate can show up. Organizing for such transient groups can be challenging.

Second, worship has potential to become inwardly focused, emphasizing creativity for self-expression alone. Worship practices are in danger of becoming articles of consumption to meet private needs or desires. People "accumulate" experiences rather than become transformed by them.

Third, insularity can lead to the development of personality cults. To address this concern, facilitators and leaders in a variety of communities studied by Gibbs and Bolger emphasize the public aspect of faithful living in different ways. They cite one church in England that protests against child labor by not allowing clothing with brand names into their worship space. Another church in the United States refuses to let technology play more than a supporting role in worship, while emphasizing relationships through conversation and prayer. A third in Scotland emphasizes art but also the public message that the art conveys so that people responding can have a communal, transformative experience around the art.[30]

Leaders in emerging churches face a fourth challenge as they initiate faith communities that reject hierarchy. They are particularly wary of charismatic CEO-pastors whom they encounter in megachurches. News headlines that detail the downfall of pastors who have no accountability structures for their lives teach emerging church leaders to think differently about leadership. Rejection of hierarchical control results in leadership-by-persuasion or negotiation in the emerging church. Leaders emphasize networks rather than hierarchies, with hopes that all participants will exhibit leadership in some way. Therefore, if participants choose not to lead, the group simply gathers for the sake of being together.

For emerging church leaders, covenant relationships that point to the realm of God set the focus rather than church structure. Mission statements and formal vision-building processes do not make sense in these groups because the emphasis on relationship yields conversations about hopes and dreams; once articulated, the community chooses whether to commit time and resources to realize its dreams. Thus, the majority of emerging churches avoid static mission statements to which newcomers are required to adhere.[31]

Some leaders, in their rejection of hierarchy, attempt to create leaderless groups, reminiscent of the 1960s.[32] However, research by Gibbs and Bolger showed that leaderless groups were not effective. Power struggles developed or people had no focus and therefore abandoned their groups until the groups could no longer sustain themselves. Rotating or fluid leadership seemed to make more sense to those interviewed by the researchers. Leaders step forward according to their passions and gifts as needs require. Once gifts are respected, leadership can be shared appropriately and the richness of community can be realized.[33] Passion and influence also motivate people to follow a particular person at any given time; the point is that the group itself, rather than an institution, gives a leader her or his status. Therefore, consensus building and facilitation of a democratically chosen agenda mark the emphases of dynamic emerging churches. More comfortable as facilitators, leaders create space and opportunity for ministry, while encouraging the development of gifts and competencies in each participant. Facilitator-leaders also consider themselves participants in collaborative, emerging ministries. If emerging churches become too large to be effective in their own participants' minds, they either create fluid leadership teams or break into smaller congregations or groups.

> They look to avoid modern forms of control at all costs. The key idea is that leaders emerge based on the activity at hand and are not the sole leaders of a group. All are welcome to the leadership table. Consensus decision-making is the norm. If a leadership team is chosen, these leaders operate as spiritual directors, mentors, and facilitators.[34]

Emerging churches evolve quickly as networks. With the popularity and speed of the Internet and the emphasis on experiential community, these churches have made inroads with disillusioned, former traditional church members and unchurched populations alike. Indeed, many emerging church leaders come from traditional, conservative evangelical church backgrounds themselves. They protest against fundamentalist rigidity and organizational structures with formulaic solutions to life's problems in these churches. Spiritual isolationism and reductionism, described by emerging church leaders in D.A. Carson's *Becoming Conversant with the Emerging Church,* troubled these leaders before they left their churches.[35] As a result, leaders use different modes of Internet communication to invite people into community in a nonthreatening, low-risk way. The emphasis on experience makes these churches attractive:

> [O]ne reason why the movement has mushroomed so quickly is that it is bringing to focus a lot of hazy perceptions already widely circulating in the culture. It is articulating crisply and polemically what many pastors and others were already beginning to think, even though they did not enjoy—until the leaders of this movement came along—any champions who put their amorphous malaise into perspective.[36]

At a deeper level, emerging churches attempt to create ministries that reach postmoderns, who in turn are motivated to reach out to the world.

Implications for the Mainline Church

The critique of both the mainline churches and evangelical megachurches by emerging churches shows a strong indication that individual faith communities are willing to reject institutional forms of church. They also reject authoritarian leadership in megachurches and preconstructed liturgies found in the mainline churches. The underlying issues critique linear, logical approaches to faith development and formulaic understandings of theology and governance. Emerging churches, however, do not reject the importance of faith communities and their ability to make an impact in the world. Rather than attempting to reform the church, emerging churches understand themselves as rejecting institutions and, at the same time, recreating understandings of what it means to be church.

However, despite the use of innovative technologies, the current emerging movement itself is not new: church and denominational splits throughout history resulted from critique of the parent churches. For example, Martin Luther and contemporaries called for Roman Catholic Church reform in protest against institutional practices at the time of the Reformation. Most mainline denominations can diagram their histories, noting theological or doctrinal disagreements causing new movements to form from parent churches.

Emerging churches also are in danger of making scripture, tradition, reason, and experience so relative that very little foundational faith remains rooted in understanding rich Christian tradition and theology. Subsuming careful exegesis of the scriptures and lessons learned throughout Christian history to experiential meaning alone reduces the emerging church to reinventing a movement in reaction to its own past. Then, it is in danger of becoming disconnected from its heritage while living with the illusion that utilizing ancient rituals, without contextual study or comprehension, keeps the emerging church grounded. To reject rationalism by prizing experience above all is simply the swing of a pendulum. Instead, intellectual inquiry combined with experiential faith feeds human beings on a holistic level, keeping them rooted in tradition rather than reacting against institutions, calling them into future adventures of faith.

A unique opportunity exists for the mainline church in this age. The church can celebrate its rich history by teaching persons how theological thinking in each epoch led to particular doctrines. At the same time, the church can invite conversation about what theological work needs to be done in the present to co-create with God God's realm in the world. Both experience and understanding, insofar as one can understand the Divine, balance the life of the mind with the heart and soul. Embracing postmodern entrepreneurial mindsets can contribute creatively to theological work. Apprehending God's work and purposes through theological study and reflection opens possibilities for understanding that cannot be reached by experience alone.

The mainline church also can begin to think of itself as a movement again, grounded in the great commandment as its foundational story, ready to live this word in the particular contexts relevant to current local and global needs. Finally, the mainline church can rethink its own nature and purpose rather than abandoning it to create disaffected communities. It no longer has to "make" disciples by requiring people to conform to set criteria. It can claim new life with those who are marginalized by the negative effects of globalized consumerism. Indeed, the post-Christendom mainline can create its future from the very margins to which it is called as a voice for those most in need of hope and love.

REFLECTION QUESTIONS

1. What postmodern characteristics do the local churches exhibit? What impact does the "experience economy" make on the local church?
2. How does the mainline church's understanding of paid professional leadership help or harm its congregational life? Is there an alternative way for trained theologians to lead the churches?
3. What would a "bridge conversation" look like between modern and postmodern understandings of the role of the church, its worship, and its doctrines?

PART II

Creating Process-Church

5

Foundations for Process-Church

*If we dare to move through our fear, to practice knowing as
a form of love, we might abandon our illusion of control and
enter a partnership with the otherness of the world.*

PARKER PALMER[1]

The Western mainline church exists in a post-Christendom world
that is globalizing quickly. The church finds itself negotiating the
complexity of both modern and postmodern mindsets. Knowing
current contexts in which the church lives provides essential
information for the potential of the mainline church's ministry in
the future. Fear of decline can indeed be transformed into hope of
living successfully in the gospel as community that claims new life.
This transformation is not automatic, nor is it likely to result from
a quick-fix solution.

The problem before the church is both spiritual and theological
in nature. Therefore, transformation requires spiritual and theological
work. The emphasis on self-preservation or growth as success, set by
secular standards, raises the question about a community's call in
ministry. This emphasis is not only spiritual, but also theological:
churches functioning as lifestyle enclaves or pseudo-civic organizations
miss the point of being the body of Christ called to share the good

news of wholeness and love. A theological outlook that embraces God's relationship invested in an evolving creation as the way by which a "new thing" is happening claims the hope of the gospel and the hope of the church.[2] Theological work challenges the church to change from a self-preserving institution struggling to survive to a spiritually dynamic, organized movement that constantly claims new life as the future unfolds.

Historical and Theological Foundations

Pursuing the hope of new life requires that churches engage their own participants differently than church growth packages or purpose-driven programs prescribe. The invitation here is to begin to think about Christian community in a new light, based on the foundational scriptural text introduced earlier: the great commandment. This command (to love God with all of one's being and to love neighbor as self) frames who Christians claim to be. Grounding conversation about the future of the church in the great commandment sets the stage for a new kind of journey. By inviting persons into exploratory space about the nature of Christianity based on this foundational premise, church leaders introduce an opportunity to engage tradition through study of specific texts, historical and theological understandings of their origin and messages for their time, and in-depth conversation of the texts' meanings for the current day. Theological reflection is a crucial component for the process of claiming new life.

This process-based journey, as opposed to a destination-based one, moves established, modernist congregations from a desperate desire to return to the "glory days" of the past to a present-future continuum that embraces flexibility and adventure. For postmodern explorers of the faith, the journey metaphor meets the need to find meaning in a complex and, at times, hostile world, while also focusing beyond oneself to create community that makes a difference in the world. Postmodern persons seek to combine an ancient understanding of spiritual life, particularly in wilderness times, with a new means of its expression. This journey through the wilderness intentionally creates sacred space to do so.

The process perspective represented here is based on the earlier work in process philosophy and metaphysics of Alfred North Whitehead (1861–1947) and modified by the philosophical thought of Charles Hartshorne (1897–2000). The nuances in their arguments about the nature of God provide distinctions in their thought, but they both maintain that what is real or alive is always in process. To be static is to be dead, past, or abstract. So, to be alive, or actual, means that each moment of existence is one point in a matrix of events. Each moment responds to its past and to its environment, which lures this moment into what is possible for it to become. In other words, what is living responds to a past and also moves toward future occasions to which it can contribute. For example, no absolutely independent individuals exist; individuals become who they are now based on their past. Their present influences their future. So, past events are integrated into events of the present, which are taken up by future events.[3]

Process thought emphasizes the developmental nature of reality: becoming rather than being. Reality ultimately is made up of experiential events rather than static objects or rules. As individuals are in process, they integrate past with present with future while simultaneously relating to others. Thus, there is a sequence of integrations at every moment on many levels of connection. Terms such as "interrelatedness," "unity in diversity," "mutual transformation," and "non-dualism" exemplify the relational aspect of process thought.[4]

Process theology appropriates this philosophical thought by claiming that the ultimate power is to practice the lure of love, drawing relationship to it rather than coercing relationship to some predetermined end. Therefore, Whitehead would connect process thought to process theology this way: God, Ultimate Power, is One who works slowly and quietly through love, affected by as well as affecting what happens in the world. Therefore, God is the great companion who suffers together with creation while calling creation forth with an eternal lure as it advances into its possibility. Because God is affected by love, God's actions are changeable.[5]

Hartshorne's focus on process thought addresses the contradiction of orthodoxy's absolute, unchanging God with the changing, relational, responsive God by describing how these notions of God live in tension together. He claims that God's love is absolute, necessary, and unchanging; God's relationship with creation is one of pure love. Expressions of that love, not love itself, are relative to and change with the current state of creation and its circumstances, providing relationship to creation that is the most fruitful. Therefore, God affects creation and responds to it. God's perfection and power are unsurpassable by anything other than God. At the same time, all that occurs in creation affects God. In God's involvement in the passage of time, God embraces more awareness and new ways of being in relationship with creation as new possibilities show themselves in creation itself. For Hartshorne then, God's existence as love remains absolute, while the character of God's loving relationship to creation is relative to the state of creation at any given occasion.[6] Another way to phrase this understanding of God is to use process theologian John Cobb's words: God is a "creative-responsive love."[7]

The primary principle of process theology focuses on the God-creation relationship based in love. Introducing the nature and mission of the church in the midst of this theological perspective necessarily connects the lure of love as the process by which the church's role unfolds from the past, to the present, and into the future. Referring to the great commandment as a foundational text about the God-creation relationship based in love leads the way for developing an understanding of church-in-process, or Process-Church. Marjorie Hewitt Suchocki, an Emeritus Professor of Theology at Claremont School of Theology who wrote *God, Christ, Church: A Practical Guide to Process Theology*, helps identify what such a church would look like. She briefly introduces a notion of "process ecclesiology" within the wider rubric of process theology.[8] Her theological premise is this:

> In the movement from past to future, one sees change and continuity. The change rests in the reality that there is ever a new past to be incorporated into an ever newly arising present, but the continuity rests in the fact that the present internally incorporates the influences of the past within itself. There is an essential connectedness to all existence, a togetherness in relationality that continuously moves beyond itself.[9]

For Christians, the understanding of lived faith is that human beings become extensions of the incarnation of God: Christ in the world. This connection with God through Christ brings diverse groups of people together as community with the will to follow God's lead in addressing the needs of the world around them as expressed by Jesus Christ. The love of Jesus was intensely responsive to his surroundings.[10]

He noticed the lepers and beggars, healing and blessing them despite their being considered unclean. He blessed foreign women and challenged the rich to think about their wealth in new ways. He healed, forgave, and taught wherever he traveled, paying attention to those who normally remained invisible in or untouchable to the crowds. His teachings were contextual, telling fisher folk to fish for people and farmers to sow seeds in good soil. Jesus pointed to the nature of God: love.

For a community focused on living as the incarnation of God's love in and for the world, the attention to "process" or intentional work on the evolution of the church will be crucial. The great commandment grounds the purpose of Christian community from its inception while calling participants to live into the rhythm of embracing the past, living its tenets in the present, and casting hope for the future. Suchocki describes a moving rhythm between past and future wherein the church in the present is ever formed anew. The present constitutes holy living based in love and justice.[11] This continuity with the past and essential openness to God's future requires that Christian institutions move beyond self-preservation toward ongoing attentiveness to inclusive well-being. Structures—whether churches, parachurches, or small groups—must assess continually the purpose for their existence in light of God's radical love for creation and the call to incarnate this love with each other.[12]

The apostolic nature of the early church provides an initial framework for creating Process-Church. "Apostolicity is the sense in which the church is continuously affected by and responsible to its past, beginning with the testimony of the apostles to the life, death, and resurrection of Jesus."[13] The central element here is the constant testimony about the realm of God, embodied in Jesus Christ; testimony itself includes a call to identify with Jesus Christ in the present as path toward the realm of God in the future. The heart of this witness is relational and community-oriented, where Christians themselves are embodied proclamations of the good news. The church presented in Acts 2:42 illustrates the ideal community of mutual care through the sharing of all goods for a life of well-being and accountable connection. These early Christians set the context for teaching, living in fellowship, eucharist, and prayer. Their lives were based on the foundational message of God's love embodied in Jesus

Christ, and they were able to proclaim the good news wherever they went. As they witnessed to their faith, they were changed by the very message they proclaimed, thus remaining anchored in the foundation while going forth, evolving into new life.

Rather than creating a rule of success to impose on every community, the apostolic notion proclaims a love of God that makes the most sense in particular contexts, changing in its manifestation but unchanging in its intent. Today for example, advocating and working for justice that promotes well-being looks different in Mexico City than it does in South Dakota, Beijing, Darfur, or Baghdad. The succession of witnesses to the good news provides an evolving understanding of what responses to God's love look like. In middle-class suburbia, for example, the issue next door may be domestic violence. In Darfur, the issue next door may be safety, food, and water. The foundation for response in love is the same: Christians know God's love and reach out to neighbor in that same love. The response itself is particular to the need, but the motive for response remains constant. Christian faith may be proclaimed in every culture and context with love as the universal norm, but can only be transformative if the proclamation and accompanying action is relative to the particularities of each culture and context.

In addition to reclaiming the character of apostolicity, Process-Church understands its purpose as the co-creator of the realm of God in the world. This realm has at its center the well-being of human beings and creation itself. The controversial aspect of a process theology that presupposes the possibility of God and humanity sharing the creation of a future is that it assumes that God changes and adapts to circumstances, always transforming them to point toward the holy realm that is possible even as the journey shifts and changes. God puts before humanity possibilities and lures human beings always to choose love. God is actively inviting humanity toward love. Suchocki says it this way:

> We speak of one occasion, the wealth of its past, and God's feeling of that occasion and integration of the occasion with Christ in the depths of divine harmony. But the process happens again and again and again. Not one occasion, and not simply one series of occasions, but every occasion whatsoever,

is felt by God and integrated according to divine wisdom into the primordial harmony. Everything affects everything else in this process universe. God adapts aims to the world in light of this intensity of complex interrelationships. Therefore, what the church accomplishes is felt by God and dealt with by God in transforming wisdom. God blends the whole church everlastingly with that constellation we call Christ in the primordial nature of God... The effect is in the multiplicity of aims given to the individuals of the church, each aim being given in light of all the others. Thus, the very aims of God, reflecting the divine holiness of the church, tend toward a communal form of that holiness on earth.[14]

Process theology, therefore, introduces a God who adapts with events toward a higher aim to bring about community that nourishes humanity and creation. This notion challenges orthodox understandings of God, namely that God is unchangeable and is driving time and space in a linear fashion toward an ultimate endpoint where God will make all things new without human participation. Instead, God invites persons to co-create the future with God, so that creation has a unified aim: God's unfolding purpose.

One example that explains the premise of process theology can be seen in interpretations of the crucifixion and resurrection. Suchocki and John Cobb understand the resurrection as a unique event that matters for humanity's well-being, which God used as response to the human political act of Jesus' crucifixion. For Suchocki and Cobb, the crucifixion/resurrection event was the greatest opportunity for humanity to see God's aim: transforming death to life as a manifestation of loving relationship with creation. This interpretation does not claim that God "foreordained" the crucifixion to make restoration of right relationship with God (atonement) possible. Instead, human response to the crucifixion/resurrection event weaves together with divine action, co-creating a process of new, life-giving community that spreads the good news of God's love. This process does not preclude human sin, the cause of crucifixion in this case, or actions and behaviors that separate humanity from relationship with God and each other; rather, God's motive of love, seen in transforming death to life, is always offering new ways of bringing persons back into healthy relationship based in well-being for individuals and creation.

A basic understanding of process theology is important for thinking about Process-Church. Theology informs ecclesiology: notions of God's nature directly relate to notions of the nature and purpose of church as a gathering called out to be God's hands in the world.[15] If God changes action in relationship with creation, then the church as an extension of the incarnation of God in Christ also must be changeable. Better yet, the church claims the need for ongoing, intentional change to be faithful to God's constant and enduring call to love.

The Process-Church requires theological thought about the nature of God and the church, which informs the practices and foci of participants. Grounded in the great commandment, Process-Church continually reinvents itself as it understands its response to and co-creation of God's and humankind's evolving path toward wholeness and love for all people. There exists no prescription for what church looks like other than a community of the faithful who work toward the well-being of neighbors and strangers while remaining in relationship with God through worship, sacrament, study, and prayer (Acts 2:42). This assertion then challenges institutionalization of church theologically and doctrinally. It allows for faith communities to work out their own ongoing evolution of living out the gospel in the world by proclaiming God's integrating action toward a space and time where love and justice prevail.

For Process-Church, understanding of history as tradition changes from upholding routine custom or unexamined habits (traditionalism)[16] to acknowledging a rich past of transformative learning (tradition) that informs the present as it unfolds into the future.

> Tradition implies repetition, a certain kind of invariability that claims an ancient source: "assumptions, beliefs and patterns of behavior handed down form the past," the Latin tradition. However, other concepts are commonly confused—or intertwined—with tradition, such as custom, convention, routine, and endowment. In order to understand tradition in relation to congregational vitality, it is important to be able to sort out what people mean when they appeal to tradition.

Custom refers to what people do—actions in accordance with precedent; tradition refers to that which accompanies action. Customs may (and often must) change, whereas traditions are forms of belief and practice that are understood to have longer historical grounding linked to some more ancient and universal source of authority and meaning.[17]

Taking into account then the status of the post-Christendom church that lives in a fast-paced, globalizing world evolving into postmodern mindsets, the introduction of a Process-Church provides a unique means of claiming new life that is contextual, respectful of tradition, grounded in love, and capable of reaching new generations in meaningful ways.

Developing an Ethic of Inquiry

Process-Church begins at the local level, but it engages the political and social issues of the day, thinks both globally and locally, and keeps itself rooted in the great commandment. What looks like loving one's neighbor in the early twenty-first century may change significantly by mid-century. Flexibility of church work, worship, and function, even theological stance, is required for Process-Church's healthy evolution as a gathering of Christians who respond to the call to bring wholeness and love to the world.

When shifting the understanding of the nature and purpose of church from converting non-Christians to Christianity, providing a haven from the world, making disciples or finding ways to survive, leaders must invite people into sacred space, *tenemos,* and sacred time, *kairos,* for the exploration of a new future with God. Leaders will need to create a safe environment for conversation in either small groups or as a whole community about the nature and purpose of church in the midst of globalized, postmodern contexts.[18]

Essential to the task at hand is the ability of faith communities to adopt an ethos, an ongoing disposition or posture, of questioning. Creating a learning community starts with surfacing assumptions about one's current faith and context. An ethic of inquiry that not only revolves around study but engages in asking meta-questions about life and faith provides opportunity for a shift from unexamined faith constructs or naiveté about faith itself to an examination of beliefs and the nature of God's action in the world. Focused questions allow for realignment with the grounding text and examination of the church's assumptions about role and purpose. Questions also provide opportunity for self-assessment.

Eric Law provides a model for such work when he introduces the iceberg analogy of organizational culture in *Sacred Acts, Holy Change*. He encourages faith communities to look at assumptions about their attitudes and theologies by having people name their external cultures (the ice showing above the water) and their internal cultures (the ice below the water). Transformation of the church can only occur when there is profound change of the internal culture, often submerged and, therefore, largely invisible.[19] The external culture includes explicit structures, policies, and buildings. The internal culture includes assumptions, myths, beliefs, and values, which are difficult to change because they have been accepted as normal, conditioning the way people perceive and react to the world around them.[20]

> The internal culture includes the unconscious patterns that the community repeats continually. When confronted with the question why they do it, the reply is often, "We have always done it that way." There are implicit decision-making processes and unspoken rules based on deeply held values that are so deep that no one has articulated them for a long time.[21]

Law says that exposing the submerged iceberg allows congregations to have a choice about their futures, deciding whether they will continue on their current path or find a new one.[22] This kind of inquiry through analogy leads to thoughts and perspectives that have not surfaced. For example, referring to the great commandment texts in the synoptic gospels as the basis for the church's mission leads the way for a variety of conversations: who one's neighbor is, how one understands God's nature, and the dangers of privatized faith practice versus relationship-based interaction. Loving one's neighbor invites a definition of neighbor in a simultaneously privatized and global context. Moving beyond private faith into faith that must connect with the "other" invites the question, "What can I learn from you?"[23] Asking this question of another, particularly someone of a different race, culture, economic echelon, educational level, or faith tradition not only yields new openness to context, it moves one from mere toleration to curiosity, and ideally to hospitality and solidarity in diversity. One learns to love one's neighbor through relationship. One also learns the impact of encountering the "other" and begins to find the blessing of diversity as an aspect of God's nature.

This realignment of text interpretation and resulting behavior requires courage and honesty. However, for persons to move into the *tenemos* and *kairos* where this deep work can be done with any degree of success, they must be able to face, if not challenge, the messages that denominations or church boards have created based on an anxious desire to save the church from decline. Focusing less on this anxiety and more on call reorients people to honest inquiry. In addition, people who struggle with the postmodern openness to other faiths must also encounter their own modernist assumption that Christianity is the only way for all people to be in right relationship with God. Akin to this assumption is the desire to hold on to the illusion that Christendom can be reestablished as the proper status for the church, the institutional Christian lens through which civic society should function. Only authentic inquiry in safe spaces can open conversation about these assumptions.

As living into the story of the great commandment deepens, the community engaged in study and inquiry-based conversation shifts from a culture of teaching the world what discipleship means, to learning what it means to be in a life-giving process of growing faith. The corresponding shift is that this community becomes process-based rather than institutional-based, rejecting secular notions of the definition of "successful" church while exploring possibilities of what church could mean to the world. For example, for those who understand the church as a prophetic voice on the margins of society, caring for the marginalized begins to take on new depth as the process of inquiry unfolds.

Questions about assumptions lead the way for developing an ethic of inquiry that becomes increasingly ingrained in the work of the faith community together. This ethic develops an intentional ethos of living into questions about faith constructs and simultaneous questions about the meaning of the church's foundational text. The great commandment continually calls Christians into ever-changing community based on promoting the well-being of others. Inquiry not only examines the foundational biblical text and spends time looking at assumptions, it introduces the need for theological reflection on one's work and context.

Theological Reflection

Theological reflection opens people to encountering an event or situation with particular questions about the presence and nature of God, illumining how Christians are to live in the present context. Reflection also encompasses a perception of the unfolding purposes of God through history, intersecting with creation. Careful consideration of God's interaction with creation guides one's understanding of God's nature and intent in the events of the world, which leads to particular responsive action by human beings. For Christians, theological reflection on the nature of God occurs when the scriptural story, experience, reason, and history connect. How does God relate to creation? How does creation connect with God who reconnects again with creation? Do the stories differ in the Hebrew Scriptures and New Testament regarding God's interaction with humanity? What is the role of the human being in the presence of suffering and evil? What choices for love and wholeness are before humanity in present circumstances? These theological questions are starting points for knowing God in and through evolving creation.

Intentional, disciplined theological reflection on the events of each day creates opportunity for persons to ask particular questions such as, "What does God want in this time and place?" "What is the appropriate response to the ills of society in our midst and who will respond how?" "What does love of neighbor and stranger mean in this situation?" These kinds of questions and others stemming from them lead to rich conversation about the purpose of church. As responses become more attuned to the depth of the great commandment while pointing outward to the desire of God for wholeness in today's world, the church begins to progress into its own call. Worship changes as the community takes ownership of its own response to loving neighbor. Pastoral care and social action widen to include those who live and work in proximity to the church rather than solely within it. Advocacy for change broadens to arenas beyond local and national politics as movements form to lighten the burden of those who live on the margins. Church participants gain energy and focus from their own theological and spiritual work. Concern about numbers of attendees and paying the bills lessens as the burning issues of life come to the fore. People respond to the lure of God into the future. God does not force the church toward divine purpose, but waits upon faith communities to discover the possibilities already present. As congregations develop an ethic of inquiry, their imaginations begin to work on what might be evolving as an aim particular for this time and place and they set out to co-create the future with God.

REFLECTION QUESTIONS

1. What does the local congregation think the purpose of the church is? How does the community begin to discern God's call?

2. How does the idea of changing the focus of the local church affect the congregation? What choices will be necessary and how will change occur, if at all?

3. What role does imagination have in the life of faith? How is it possible to have faith grounded in scripture and also use imagination?

6

Imagining the Church of the Future
A Method

Spirituality is more than churchgoing. It is possible to go to church and never develop a spirituality at all. Spirituality is the way in which we express a living faith in a real world. Spirituality is the sum total of attitudes and actions that define our life of faith.

JOAN CHITTISTER[1]

In the midst of *tenemos* and *kairos,* sacred spaces and times created for the work of examining assumptions and asking questions of theological and spiritual significance, a new energy begins to emerge. Participants begin to see beyond their own spiritual needs and join in a journey that can be described as a grand adventure. Adventurers are people who undertake uncertain yet exciting journeys into the unknown, eager to see what lies ahead. However, they also know that the adventure is not without some hardship, pain, and disappointment. Those willing to travel new paths will encounter unfamiliar wilderness where the way forward remains obscure for a time. Occasional dead-ends can lead to critics claiming, "See, I told you it wouldn't work." Nonetheless, a faith communion begins to form, a *koinonia,*[2] based on people orienting their lives toward God's faithful love. It is a *koinonia* of faith, hope, and love, with these three gifts defining one another.

As the ethic of inquiry deepens through theological reflection on the great commandment and the observation of local context, people orient themselves in a new way toward their own community and to the world; imaginings about the nature of church and its future begin to enter the conversation. Questions of potential for the church's presence in the world become pressing. At this point in the emerging *koinonia* arises an opportunity for leaders to invite participants to engage in intentional exercises of imagination. Having thought through the church's foundational mission (to be in relationship with God and neighbor as defined by love), having surfaced assumptions about past understandings of the nature and role of church, and having explored context in terms of the impact of globalization and postmodern challenges, the church is now ready to re-vision its work. Thus, the ethic of inquiry moves to another level by creating scenarios of possibility for the future church.

The Long View

The postmodern challenge for the post-Christendom church, namely attention to meaning found through authentic experience, combined with a globalized context, provide important input for exercises of imagination about the future of the church. As the church reflects on its own purpose and the context in which it is called to carry out this purpose, its participants come to a place where they need to synthesize observations, experiences, and insights. With an emphasis on discipline and questions about passion, focus, and momentum-building energy in mind, participants in the following exercise move from reflection to active imagination about co-creating new life for ministry in their contexts.

A question to bear in mind when entering into this particular process is a simple one: "What issues keep people up at night?" Another angle might be, "What is the church community passionate about?" Professor Jim Collins uses these questions both for businesses and the social sector.[3] Collins provides a preparatory rubric for subsequent scenario-building by claiming that disciplined people, disciplined thought, and disciplined action are essential for co-creating an organization, in this case church, into a healthy, vital body of Christ making a difference in the world. Collins's emphasis on discipline speaks to the church, where an understanding of the importance of spiritual discipline in particular is not a new one. Discipline in this case means intentionally attending to the questions and challenges facing the church. It also means that persons engaging in the conversation are invested in the spiritual work required for reorienting the church's understanding of success. Without discipline and long-term focused attention on the evolution of the church in the midst of God's divine purposes, it is unlikely that much meaningful change can occur.

Collins points out that leaders themselves must have a passionate desire and will to invite organizations into a new place. They surround themselves with a particular group of people who are willing to contribute energy and skill, disciplined for the work of change. This group faces the facts of the status quo, with the option to use Eric Law's iceberg exercise[4] to aid them in understanding implicit cultural and behavioral assumptions. Disciplined thought is crucial at this stage. Collins calls this "confronting the brutal facts" while retaining the unwavering faith that in the end, the good news will prevail.[5] As this group of disciplined thinkers recognizes the difficulties they are facing, they turn to Collins's most important concept adapted for the church: doing those things that the church is best at doing and letting everything else go. This focus helps congregations in identifying the type of faithful work they want to do in response to the great commandment by asking (1) what the local church is deeply passionate about, (2) what the church can be the best at, and (3) what best drives the church's resources. Collins explains that churches begin with passion, then refine passion with a rigorous assessment of what they can contribute best to the communities they touch. Then they create a way to tie their resources directly to passion and gifts for ministry.[6]

Collins has created three foci to aid the church in identifying its strengths, passions, and resources to be used for niche ministries, answering the call to be present where there is the most need for love in the world. These foci challenge the church to think about its future in a disciplined manner, helping people intentionally focus on what ministries matter and how to point the faith community to its call with a passionate response. People take on responsibility for ministry with patience and fortitude, looking for signposts of God's unfolding purposes, co-creating a momentum of ministry that eventually takes on a life of its own that is larger than the church itself.[7]

The stage is set for the disciplined work of the church by defining skills, passions, and call. Combining emphases on strengths, passions, and resources with a method for scenario-building based on disciplined thought introduces a strong process methodology that moves the church from static institution to Process-Church. Those who choose to align with God's call, having named the brutal facts and the passions available to them already, can turn next to Peter Schwartz's specific process for mining current context and past trends for clues about the future.[8] Schwartz's framework applied to the church complements Collins's emphases by drawing the church into process-orientation through specific lenses relevant to the church's particular context.

Schwartz, though a business expert rather than a church consultant, provides a process by which any organization can create educated scenarios about the future and then learn to move into the future that emerges. The process employed for the local church's purposes adapts Schwartz's methodology for a church that increasingly is called to be countercultural. Use of imagination to create scenarios for local churches is not responding to economic and attendance pressures, but is providing good news in the midst of complex contexts where aspects of globalization and commodification of all life have resulted in human and environmental damage.

Schwartz describes "scenario" as a way to organize perceptions about alternative future environments in which decisions might be played out.[9] Scenario-builders think and dream in a disciplined way about the future. The impact of such an organized, yet open-ended process is the ability to act with a "knowledgeable sense of risk" and reward that separates wise leaders from bureaucrats or gamblers.[10] These scenarios are not predictions about the future but intentional decisions based on an open-minded response to God's call for the church. The essential component is to move beyond "right and wrong" thinking into possibility thinking outside of mental prearrangements. Scenario-building is the opposite of living in denial. Instead, it reorients persons' radars, encouraging attention to contexts, perceptions, and feelings of the local church's place in the world around them. The key behind working with scenarios is to attune persons involved in the process to multiple points of view and an acceptance of uncertainty.

Schwartz notes that those most easily attuned to scenario-building are persons who have made mistakes in their own lives and have demonstrated that they have learned from them. Participants in scenario-building exercises need to be chosen carefully. Those who will contribute to the process in a disciplined manner are of great importance for the depth of the process itself. The process is a long-term, high-energy commitment, requiring people to conduct research about their contexts. Each person must be able to gather information and participate well in a group dynamic. A facilitator or leader from outside the local church can consult with the minister to determine who might be likely candidates for such work. Participants should include a variety of persons, church insiders and at least one outsider, from a variety of backgrounds if possible. The creative process is most effective when the perspectives involved differ significantly.[11]

Having chosen dedicated members for the scenario-building group, facilitators invite them to conduct informal research on a variety of topics at several levels of inquiry: movements in the church locally, nationally, and globally; denominational trends; the impact of post-Christendom cultures; worldwide economic, political, and technological movements; postmodern emphases; and the role of the gospel in each. This information not only creates understanding of context, it also provides insight to important trends.

Then Schwartz adds another, often forgotten component. He calls for scenario-builders to pay attention to events occurring outside of mainstream society. "Innovation is the center's weakness. The structure, the power and the institutional inertia all tend to inhibit innovative thinkers and drive them to the fringes. At the social and intellectual fringes, thinkers are freer to let their imaginations roam, but are still constrained by the sense of current reality."[12] Paying attention to remarkable people and sources of surprise provides clues about what is happening on the fringes, the margins of church and society.

Cultural exegesis, the critical study of culture, also provides insight into the information needed before entering the scenario-building exercise. How does the good news of the gospel connect currently with the culture, if at all? How does the local church differ from or mimic the culture? These questions help participants begin to assess the connections between churches and cultures.

In an environment where cultural change has accelerated beyond all cultural expectations, cultural exegesis is one of the most critical tools the church can use as it moves into the future. Careful study of the emerging culture can help shift our focus from fears of a culture-corrupted gospel to more productive questions of how our cultural insensitivities expand or obscure our understanding of a gospel that is simultaneously real, concrete, and practical, yet also infinite and mysterious.[13]

This level of research appears daunting at first glance. However, information acquired from research has significant bearing on building scenarios. The expectation is not so much to write a treatise based on findings but to accumulate a wide understanding of global and local contexts and trends. Noting the emphases of news stories, listening to a younger generation's view of the meaning of life, reading foreign newspapers online, watching preachers on television, asking colleagues' opinions about current national political decisions, or simply watching the costs of energy all constitute important information for scenario-building. Organizing information into categories such as economy, culture, politics, theology, or demography helps simplify the task.

The research step, in scenario-building elicits resistance in congregations that have never thought about their contexts in an intentional way before. Some churches will pursue this endeavor more thoroughly than others. The key is to include people who demonstrate good observation skills and an ability to articulate their findings, whether they are local stories or quantitative data, in a way that contributes to the scenario-building process described below. Intentionality and thoroughness are the most important factors in this type of research.

The remainder of the scenario work allows for speculation and imagination to be integrated into the research findings, thereby moving scenario-builders from data-driven reactions to imaginative responses. Schwartz indicates this integration has resulted in consistent outcomes during his own consultancy work. Scenarios, once created, usually and unwittingly categorize themselves into three emphases: (1) current situations continue and emerge slightly better than their present state, (2) situations become worse leading to decay and depression, and (3) situations become significantly different and better, based on fundamental change.[14] The first two emphases produce incremental change and the last one establishes a major discontinuity with the present, showing potential for transformation. The reality that unfolds may be a combination of the three, so it is important for participants to keep all scenarios in mind. Schwartz recommends building only three or at most, four, scenarios so that as the future unfolds, clarity of direction is identified more easily.[15]

Scenario-building

Before scenario-building begins, preparatory work for the entire congregation needs to occur. Preparatory work for the church involves the whole congregation in the process at different points, thereby making the endeavor to move toward transformation owned by everyone. This design for preparatory work differs from business models because it places power and accountability for the church's future directly into the hands of church participants. This design also differs from the emerging church's propensity to "wait and see what happens" because it provides a method in which members actively and intentionally engage to claim new life without rejecting their church structures altogether. Once congregations have affirmed the process that has been made as transparent as possible, they are ready to work alongside the scenario-builders.

The flow of scenario-building for the church can be outlined in seven steps.[16] Each step provides one component of a method that changes the mindset of institutional churches from living in survival mode to becoming transformative agents in the world. Motivation to do this work comes when churches are acknowledging that the wilderness is not meant to be a permanent setting for the faithful. Wilderness provides opportunity to learn about one's surroundings and also test hope. Yet wilderness experiences become deadly if wanderers remain passive about their own progress on the journey. Only those who set their sights to a new land will pursue the future in hope.

In the preparatory work and seven steps outlined here, Corner Church reappears from chapter 1 as an example of how scenario-building works to shift churches from survival to ongoing transformation on a practical level. Corner Church is poised to transition into a Process-Church based on its desire to reintroduce an after-school ministry with children in an economically challenged neighborhood characterized by "missing" parents. If the church were to work through these process steps, it could live into an imaginative and fruitful future as a Process-Church, co-creating with God wholeness and love for its neighborhood.

Preparatory Work for the Church

Preparatory work, which must occur before scenario-building, can be as structured or as fluid as the congregation prefers.[17] Steps outlined here are a means to present information for the leader rather than as a sequential formula. The flow of the preparation can shift as the leader deems appropriate or as the conversation unfolds. Once scenario-building work begins, however, the facilitator should pay attention to the sequence of the steps as an important component of the work.

To prepare the congregation for the next eighteen months to two years of work, the minister both leads and teaches participants about the process ahead. To do so, first the minister invites members to "confront the brutal facts" together regarding their church's situation. If current trends continue in the church, what will happen in the next six months? In the next year? In the next five years? What kinds of resources does the church have and use? What does the local neighborhood look like and how will it affect the church in the short and long term? What is happening with financial support in the church? Is there conflict in the church that has not been dealt with in a healthy manner? How is the morale of the minister (and/ or the staff)? These questions may serve to depress everyone for the time being, but they also are necessary to paint a realistic picture of the state of the church.

Second, the minister introduces an ethic of inquiry by teaching congregants how to reflect theologically on the nature of the church's ministry.[18] As participants think about what it means to be Christian in relationship with God and each other, they begin to name what is important for them as children of God. So, the ethic of inquiry begins with theological reflection, orienting participants to their deepest-held faith claim and grounding them in their Christian identities. Developing the ethic of inquiry will require several months of conversation with the congregation through small group studies, at meetings, and in worship. Teaching people how to think theologically is itself a lifetime task.

The third step for the congregation's preparation also invokes an ethic of inquiry, but at a different level. The minister invites the congregation to think about its external and internal cultures with the aid of the iceberg analogy. Participants name what is immediately noticeable to visitors as the external culture. The internal culture—with its assumptions, myths, and unquestioned behaviors—takes more time to reveal. Work on these observations will take several months and can occur concurrently with the previous two steps. Scenario-builders will want to take note of the conversation for their discussions later.

Fourth, the minister invites the congregation to name what energy and passion they might have for particular ministries. Specifically questioning what issues keep people up at night can yield some discussion about deeply felt needs people wish to address. It also may be that members cannot name passions at this time because they have succumbed to worry, fear, or depression about the future of the church. However, if there are passions named, then this information can be useful to the scenario-building group as they develop the church's focal issue in their own process.

The fifth component for preparation combines the first four through study of the great commandment in the gospel texts. Facing the facts about the church's status and also naming its internal culture, while theologically reflecting on these subjects in light of the great commandment, illicit self-assessment and perhaps stirrings of a vision for the future. Focus on the great commandment and its pertinence for ministry in the local context creates an openness to imagine the future. At this point, when energy is rising, the minister introduces a sixth step, identifying the specific components of the scenario-building process to the congregants with an eye toward transformative work. He or she invites the congregation to be part of the process as the small group does its work, supplying information and ideas at various stages. In the seventh and related step, the minister also warns of the encroaching wilderness time that may feel like chaos to some.

It helps the church to be forewarned that everyone is about to enter a wilderness adventure of a new kind, which will require patience and care for each other. The minister assures the congregation that the wilderness is necessary for the transformative journey with God into the future.

Finally, the minister identifies scenario-building group members to the congregation, indicating that this group will be having regular conversations about their work with members so that their process is as transparent as possible. This conversation is not to seek affirmation for reaching particular conclusions in the process, but to share information between the rest of the congregation and the scenario-builders.

Throughout the preparatory work, the minister and other church leaders incorporate the insights gleaned into worship, study, prayer, and meetings with the congregation. Inquiry evolves as an ethos in the whole life of the church. Evidence of the congregation's work shows itself in its life together.

Preparation for the Scenario-building Group

The minister and a facilitator, who is a colleague or denominational leader external to the church, choose a small group with members able to be disciplined in the scenario-building process. One participant needs to be someone who does not attend the church. These group members need to commit twelve to eighteen months of their time for meeting and conversation. After that time period, they join the congregation for the final step of the process. The scenario-builders can be chosen any time after the minister knows that the congregation is willing to commit to the two-year process.

The facilitator gathers the small group, including the minister, and orients them to the purpose and method of scenario-building. She or he sets timelines and expectations for the group members and invites everyone to surround the work with prayer.

Corner Church provides an illustration for preparatory work at this point. Church members already have conducted preparatory work with implicit theological reflection. By answering the question, "Who is my neighbor?" they established an outreach ministry to local children in need. Love of God and neighbor translated to members working with young persons who presented themselves at the door of the church.

Further theological reflection identifies abundance and scarcity as concerns that frame this ministry. While the church itself had little money to spare, its members chose to invest what they had in building maintenance and care for children in need. Members took seriously the biblical injunction to love neighbor by addressing the economic disparities and social concerns in the nearby neighborhoods. Indeed, Corner Church saw how proximate to poverty and crime its members lived, making a choice to address scarcity by alleviating need as best they could. Corner Church's reputation as a safe place for at-risk children resulted from this ministry.

Brokenness and wholeness also suggest themselves as theological issues related to this children's ministry. Children in their early teens who care for two or three siblings in the absences of parents or guardians, often in living conditions that promote ill health, speak of brokenness on many levels. Social issues such as poverty, lack of living wages in the job market, and availability of mind-altering substances in the midst of unhealthy, even dangerous, living conditions add together to paint a bleak picture for the future of these children. Hope in the midst of brokenness became a focus for ministry years ago at Corner Church. Wholeness came in moments when children were fed and felt cared for, though an overall sense of wholeness for children would have required a community network of childcare, feeding programs, and foster parents who encouraged school attendance and worked on literacy issues at home. Brokenness continues to be the challenge, keeping a number of church members up at night.

These issues give rise to the notion of how the church lives into the world, responding to its call to love God and neighbor as self. As the body of Christ, Corner Church lived "good news" by responding to immediate needs in concrete ways. The body of Christ pays attention to the parts of the body, not only internally, but through its connections externally as well. Working toward abundance and wholeness in the midst of scarcity and brokenness (wilderness) gives witness to the radical love that brings the realm of God closer to a fragmented, disconnected creation. In this case, Corner Church took its call seriously and worked to bring greater wholeness and health to children. The members, however, could not sustain the ministry without further input of resources to address growing needs. This "brutal fact" caused them to let go of their connection with area children. Yet the generosity of spirit provides a starting place for imagining the future despite limited resources. In the scenario-building process the chosen facilitator invites Corner Church's identified scenario-builders to move forward into the process of discerning God's future purposes.

Seven Steps for Scenario-building

Step One: Name the focal issue

Focal issues are those matters that significantly affect local populations and their environments. To name the focal issue before the local church, the facilitator poses questions to the scenario-building group that lead them eventually to identify the passion, the niche, or the challenge that the church is called to address. The questions that resonate within the group based on the preparatory work with the congregation are likely to become identifiers for a focal issue. For example, answering the question, "What does secular society have to do with the church?" can lead scenario-builders toward defining a focal issue as they struggle with the question. Learning about globalization and post-Christendom in Part One provides some insight for the group into the context in which the mainline finds itself. Responses that arise from observations about the world and the sense of what keeps participants up at night in light of these observations can frame a focal issue.

Questions with theological and ecclesiological foci that to help clarify the focal issue might include the following:

- What are the issues that keep church members up at night? What is the greatest concern of the church regarding issues of the day? Discussion about what group members heard during preparatory work with the congregation guides answers to these questions.
- How does God invite the church to participate in God's realm outside church walls? What does the phrase "interconnectedness

of all creation" mean? How would the church describe God's creative work in the world? Understandings of the great commandment and texts describing Jesus' ministry may link these concerns to current events.

- What does success in ministry look like? What does failure in ministry look like? What influences success or failure? How might Jesus answer such questions? Concerns about denominational or internal pressures can be aired.

- How does war affect local communities at home and in other nations? How do Christians think about war in light of the great commandment? Churches around the globe have the opportunity to share stories about politics of war and its wide-ranging economic and social repercussions via the Internet.

- What does the group know of the environmental crisis? How does God's hope for creation speak to human interaction with the environment? Discussion about local and national consumption of natural resources leads to a new consciousness about melting ice around the globe and subsequent fresh water availability and island/coastal land loss.

- How do economics affect the church? What does stewardship mean broadly and also in terms of economics? Members find their own jobs at risk, giving depends on both perceptions and realities of disposable income, and focus of giving is shifted from maintaining buildings to "making a difference in the world."

- What does technology have to do with the future of the church? This question pushes churches to think beyond technological tools used in worship and church meetings into exploring how Christians or explorers on the fringes are encountering active international church communities on the Internet. "Virtual church,"[19] with its international participation, may be the preference of young people or people who do not find the local church's worship meaningful.

These sample questions exemplify the kinds of discourse possible in communities of faith that are willing to embark upon a journey of change. Such reflection invites theological conversation about the purpose of church in the local community and the purpose of church in the wider workings of the world. Compiling and reflecting on these questions takes time and requires that groups gathered for scenario-building can identify what they need to know about local and global contexts and how to interpret the information. By the end of this first step, with the help of a facilitator, participants begin to name the focal issue for their particular church context.

The focal issue for Corner Church has been identified for some time. Members with few resources wish to respond to the call to love neighbor by reaching local children in need while sustaining their own lives in a holistic manner.

Step Two: Conduct research about the church's present context

In this step, Schwartz calls for attention to "predetermined elements," or "what we know we know."[20] These elements simply are documented events and data collected over a period of two to six months. What is the information needed for a wide view of society surrounding and affecting the church? Understanding globalization, post-Christendom, and postmodernism is particularly important for this step. Attention to data also informs local congregations about their contexts. People hear this kind of information in the news or read about it in printed material or on the Internet. Data might look like the following examples:

- In the United States, it is clear that mainline churches are declining in membership, attendance, and giving, though there are churches that continue to thrive.
- Church real estate can be an asset, but it also constrains economic energy and time because of the need to maintain property.
- Many young adults are searching for spiritual experiences in small groups.
- Older youth and young adults often leave church in their late teens or early twenties. If they return at all, it is because they have married, have had children, and wish to bring up their children in what they perceive to be a moral learning environment.
- Cost of living is increasing and the poverty level is also rising, so a significant portion of the population has less or no disposable income.
- People are living longer and, therefore, there is a significant strain on health care systems.

- Because people are living longer, more generations are present at any given place and time. Therefore, there is a complex, sometimes competing set of desires and belief systems alive in society and the church.
- Middle-class populations are more careful about their incomes as they age and as the cost of living rises.
- Most people live in debt.
- Organizational loyalty is low due to transient populations and changing interests.[21]
- Urban sprawl creates suburbia and exurbia with somewhat homogeneous neighborhoods and churches.
- Technology provides a means not only for communication, but for consumption of goods at a fast pace and sharing of information at high speed.

How do these examples collected from the news or other sources of data connect with the focus questions in the first step? Economic and human relations issues already begin to emerge as an early theme in this scenario process. By Step Two, the group, through its intentional information-gathering process, begins to note the complexity of concerns surrounding the church and its constituencies.

Corner Church's scenario-building group spends several months paying attention to the news, accumulating stories (qualitative information) and data (quantitative information) that have relevance for their work. Crime rates and poverty rates in the nearby urban center yield important information about challenges faced by a significant population. Energy costs continue to rise in the area, creating greater hardship for parents who attempt to provide for their families. Commuting issues concern low-income workers as costs for public transport reflect higher prices for fuel. Child truancy, living conditions, levels of disparity between rich and poor, minimum wage, and interaction of city officials with social agencies and justice movements all provide data for Corner Church's focal issue: connecting with children in need while facing minimal resources.

As the group gathers information about these concerns, the members discover the systemic relationships of the issues facing their neighbors. They spend time together organizing their research findings into broad categories and then share the data with the congregation as a regular update.

Step Three: Determine what implicit external and internal forces affect the data

Participants at this stage should pay attention to critical uncertainties, which Schwartz describes as questioning assumptions about the facts named in Step Two. The questions that frame this step are, "What factors or forces lie behind trends, facts, and perceptions in the world and in the church?" "Why is this so?" "How did they get there?" Referring to the congregation's preparatory work as they faced the "brutal facts" about the state of the local church's mission and ministry is an essential aid in answering these questions. Demographics, public opinion, recent or long-term events that live in the memory of local leaders are all forces that exist behind the facts. In this third step, the research of previous months is assessed for major trends and cycles that give some clues to the future, though they do not predict upcoming events. For instance, scenario-builders ask what lies behind declining membership and economic challenges for churches, despite a population increase in the United States. To answer this question, they can speculate about external and internal forces that are implicit (under the waterline, to use the language of the iceberg analogy). The group sets out to list forces that affect the data and the church context regarding declining membership.

An implicit, external force lying behind decreased giving statistics may be that rising poverty levels and cost-of-living rates result in less disposable income. An internal force includes the penchant for anxious churches in economic decline to reorganize themselves, "right-sizing" their staff (if they have staff), out of a desire for self-preservation. After reorganizing, churches temporarily "feel better," and inertia sets in again, causing further decline and a resulting reorganization again. People leave the church when they see that no meaningful ministry is happening, therefore adding to the downhill trend.

Another question might be how the perception of the mainline church's irrelevance became a dominant force in its own declining membership. There is room for speculation here. A variety of external and internal forces affect the notion of irrelevance. One external force appears at the economic level; middle and upper economic classes may be choosing to give any extra resources available to them to charities of their choice rather than the local church. People of means may be searching for more efficient and effective ways to make an impact on the dilemma of poverty by giving great sums to housing developments that cater to the poor and mentally challenged. They also may be giving financial aid to other countries, bypassing social agencies or government-restricted aid.

Another set of external forces regarding attendance shifts surfaces in terms of non-attendees finding new ways to meet spiritual needs. First, rather than participate on committees or listen to sermons on a weekly basis that do not address deep desires for connection with God and neighbor, they turn to counseling, spiritual direction, and small group house communities for faith development and community support. Societal trends indicate that young adults in particular avoid making commitments to organizations.[22] Church participation in rural and urban areas continues to wane and participation declines. Communities that do not respond to their local situations find themselves sidelined. Suburban churches of various sizes also experience high turnover as the job market requires frequent moves and young people relocate to college or move to urban centers for better jobs. Second, accusations of hypocrisy from those watching church leaders and members in conflict perpetuate the undesirability of the local church for those seeking spiritual input in their lives. Therefore, external forces that are not immediately evident to churches are uncovered as the group thinks through its gathered information about declining numbers and the factors behind them.

A common internal force affecting church participation, which is directly affected by external issues, manifests itself in many con-gregations: nationalism. If the group looks deeper, it may find that nationalism rises when anxiety rises. Debates about the presence of the flag in the sanctuary and singing nationalistic songs can be the fiercest of disagreements in the church during civil holidays. If a leader or a member questions public policy in a manner that differs from the majority sentiment in the church community, conversation becomes focused on this disagreement. Language also affects people. The language of war that has dominated media from the early 1990s—war on drugs, war on poverty, war on terror—sets up an "us versus them" mentality, where "we" are good and "they" are bad. War mentality provides a justification for building fences and creating protective shelters where "they" cannot infiltrate set lifestyles and beliefs. These church disagreements and even protectionisms leak into the public realm, further alienating potential church attendees.

Another internal force is the low satisfaction level in the professional ministry. Studies show that clergy and lay staff morale remains low, with some leaving the ministry altogether out of a sense of self-preservation. This occurs when clergy and laity are at odds theologically or have different workload expectations. Further, loss of respect for the profession based on news stories of clergy abuse or simply based on the perceived irrelevance of paid professional ministry contributes to low morale. One result is that fewer young people, upon hearing the stress of their elders, are interested in parish ministry and would prefer to organize their own faith communities or chaplaincies, connecting only loosely with the mainline church itself.[23]

Corner Church's scenario-building group looks at the data it has gathered over the course of two to six months and begins to ask questions about the forces behind the information gleaned from the news and from observation. Corner Church, located in an old steel industrial area, has members affected by steel mill closings since the 1970s. Economic and industrial globalization continues to affect the region as other industries follow the steel market, locating themselves in countries where cheap labor forces contribute to profit margins and few or no regulations on pollution emissions exist. Corner Church has been aware of this trend for decades. One-third of its membership was laid off by the 1980s as steel mills moved to Europe and the Far East. So issues of unemployment and underemployment with the accompanying wage, poverty, absentee parent, substance abuse, and crime statistics in the news result from a local economy that has not recovered from the loss of its primary industry.

Further, low-wage jobs remain available in the form of service industries targeting suburban populations. Low wage positions invite newly immigrated workers to locate in the urban area where housing is cheapest. Immigrants speak their own languages, creating neighborhoods where English is the second language, resulting in schools and established businesses scrambling to adapt to this new challenge. In addition, the demographics of worshiping communities change as an increasing number of different faiths are introduced to the area. Corner Church finds itself reflecting on the economy and the impact of immigration on its local context and, indeed, its own membership. Questions arise about addressing its own call as the neighborhood becomes either an enclave amidst changes around it or as the neighborhood itself changes.

Living in post-Christendom times may not seem relevant at first glance for Corner Church. However, the place of the church as an influencer, at any time in the changing urban center context and in the local neighborhood connected to it, is almost non-existent in the news. This fact reinforces the sense of irrelevance of the church for local society, firmly planting the church in the margins as a voice that does not matter. Corner Church initially did not care about having public connections as it created its own niche ministry. The issue became important as Corner Church realized it could not function indefinitely on its own. Therefore, the membership has perceived this marginalization as inevitable and succumbed to a maintenance state, characterized by tiredness and depression. The lack of church presence in the news provides information to Corner Church about its publicly perceived absence in working for wholeness and health for its neighbors. This implicit message from the world to Corner Church can prove valuable in scenario-building steps later, but also is important to acknowledge at this stage.

Finally, are there postmodern forces that impact the information gathered? Corner Church has practiced a modern understanding of church as established institution called to reach out to its neighbors and draw them into their way of being church inside their building. Therefore, at first glance, responding to issues in the news seems difficult as the world changes quickly and leaves Corner Church behind. Flexible community organizing to make an impact on social concerns in the urban world finds its way into the news. Not-for-profit agencies invent programs that open doors for the poor to make choices about their futures. Internet communication connects organizations to each other for cooperative ventures in the social sector both locally and nationally. Experimental pilot projects invite neighborhoods to create their own futures. Little of this news connects with Corner Church's faith commitment to wholeness and love for the neighborhood children to date. Understanding the scope of the work being conducted without the congregation's input provides opportunity for the church to think about its ministry in new ways.

Step Four: Rank these implicit forces by importance

Once these forces behind the data are named in Step Three, they should be ranked in level of importance based on the impact they have for the local church. What forces are important for the local church? Which ones make the most impact? Ranking these forces shows the group's emphases and helps in understanding the mindset and emotional state resulting from them. For example, if economic hardship and irrelevance of the church in daily life seem to stand out as the top two significant issues facing the church, they can be ranked accordingly. Neither issue has a ready, identifiable solution; neither alleviates the uncertainty about the future felt in most mainline churches. These critical uncertainties are necessary prerequisites for entering the next steps because they allow room for the imagination to explore possibilities rather than rely solely on facts.[24] In this case, Corner Church might rank job opportunities that provide living wages at the top, followed by the second concern: social ills that result in absentee parenthood such as substance abuse and crime.

Step Five: Develop three or four scenarios as narratives about what the future could be for the local church and community

After two to six months of information gathering and reflection upon data and its implications, the imaginative work begins. What can be imagined for the future based on the previous steps? What events may be necessary for this imagined future? Who will be important in the scenario's evolution over time? Ask this set of questions three or four times and the scenarios will arise from the group's responses.

In a hospitable climate, participants break into groups of three or four and members look far ahead into the future, playing out conversations as they come. Conversations develop new mental models and new language about the nature of the church and its mission. "Old tapes" such as, "But we have always done it this way," are rejected. Questions of identity arise and a rejection of an "official future" defined by worldly success occurs. With attention to the first four steps, scenario-builders construct three or four narratives describing possibilities for the future. These possibilities, or scenarios, are educated guesses rather than predictions. Schwartz cautions that scenario-builders are not in the business of assigning probabilities to each scenario or choosing the most likely to occur. Scenarios themselves will be both possible and surprising, breaking out of stereotypes and previously held expectations.[25]

Scenarios give attention to information gathered, events that could occur, and the players in the situations themselves. They are developed in detail, complete with specific outlines of ministries that come to mind, leaders who are most likely to be effective in each case, and an overarching understanding of reason behind the ministry, including sense of call and theological foundations informing that call. Revisiting an understanding of the great commandment in each scenario's context grounds the church's response to the future in biblical foundation. At the end of the initial scenario-building exercise, group members "sleep on" their conversations and return to it a second day. Higher creativity results when members separate for a time and let their imaginations work overnight.

Corner Church's scenario-building group develops three possibilities, which they share with the congregation.

Scenario One: Corner Church closes within five years. Former members continue to meet together as a sub-group of a larger suburban church, continuing social life in their long-held small groups. They involve themselves in mission projects already existing in the suburban church, thereby continuing to address the call to love neighbor but without overextending themselves.

Scenario Two: Corner Church maintains its level of giving and hires a part-time minister with skills in community organizing to replace Rev. Jamie. The extra money now available from a former full-time salary is put aside as seed money for a pilot project in the neighborhood. Members work with the new minister to research other urban/suburban programs to develop opportunities in neighborhood areas such as theirs. They invite suburban church members who are interested to help them create a network of social agencies, recovery program leaders, and small businesses interested in a pilot project for the neighborhood adjacent to Corner Church. This pilot project will invite parents to participate in skill-based educational opportunities conducted in the neighborhood, life-skill building partnerships with trained life-skill teachers who live locally, and after-school programs, complete with meals housed in various churches in and near the neighborhood. Parents who participate or whose children participate will be asked to return these benefits to the community by taking turns staffing after-school programs in their own neighborhood. Everyone involved who is interested in worshiping together attends a weekday service at Corner Church as schedules permit. Worship is geared toward the celebrations and trials of the neighborhood ministry and worship leadership sharing develops. Grant money from foundations and support from donors in suburban churches within the area are sought to underwrite the pilot project.

Scenario Three: A housing developer who has been acquiring land in the area decides to make an offer to Corner Church and several blocks of surrounding homes, with hopes of razing the buildings and expanding suburban neighborhoods as golf course communities. Corner Church members agree to a substantial offer and decide to attend another small church in the nearby vicinity. However, they test their vision for ministry in the local neighborhood with their potential new church home, expressing their desire to revitalize the children's ministry with the input of all the members. The sale of Corner Church will provide funding. Joining a new church will provide workers. Corner Church stipulates to the new church that this ministry is a condition of their joining; if the new church decides that it will not support such a ministry, Corner Church members will continue to search for a new house of worship. Members hope to connect with their new congregational setting and eventually integrate themselves into it, while at the same time inviting others to join them in the area ministry.

Each narrative provides a scenario significantly different than the others. One shows conditions worsening for the children's ministry because Corner Church closes altogether and children do not even have the choice of attending on Sunday. Another scenario fundamentally changes the approach to the children's ministry, increasing energy and resources geared toward developing a pilot project with the community, and changing the nature of worship dramatically. Still another scenario changes location and promotes funding, while focusing on the ministry in much the same way it functioned previously. The second scenario invites transformational change, while the other two would result in incremental change for Corner Church.

Step Six: Determine if the scenarios take into account the focal issue named in Step One

At this point, scenario-builders review the scenarios created. They then return to the first step and determine how each scenario addresses the focal issue. Which imagined futures best address the passion, niche, or challenge that the church is exploring? If the scenarios do not relate to the focal issue, then participants rework them with the focal issue in mind and without losing the scenarios' imaginative qualities.

Corner Church's scenarios can be held up against the focal issue: "members with few resources wish to respond to the call to love neighbor by reaching local children in need while sustaining their own lives in a holistic manner." The first scenario's narrative does not connect with the call to serve the neighborhood children as a way of living out Corner Church's desire to love neighbor. The ministry itself is abandoned for other ministries in a new church setting. The scenario requires little motivation or energy and succumbs to the depression and tiredness leaders feel. New life for Corner Church is not found in this possibility. The group revisits this scenario to align it with the desire expressed in the initial focus.

The second scenario finds ways to invite others into ministry with children and their families, thereby developing the community and Corner Church at the same time. Opportunities for worship together with participants in the neighborhood pilot project not only include reaching out to the stranger who is a neighbor but also inviting the stranger to be a friend. This scenario requires high motivation and energy on the part of Corner Church.

The third scenario narrative keeps the focal issue intact and provides funding for the ministry's continuance. This narrative does not expand the ministry at first glance but provides a manageable means by which the call of Corner Church can be fulfilled without the same kind of energy investment found in the second scenario. The third scenario introduces incremental change rather than transformative change.

Two scenarios address the focal issue in varying degrees, retaining the intent to reestablish neighborhood ministry as a priority. Thus, these scenarios each have potential to be successful at some level, even if the future unfolds in unexpected ways. Only the second narrative at this point leads to transformation of the church and community by providing resources and new energy for wholeness and health. However, these scenarios are not set in stone. Corner Church has more work to do before making decisions about its ministry. The final step helps shape the future. New opportunities still can emerge that alter the scenarios in helpful ways.

Step Seven: Watch the unfolding future for signposts and indications

This step is counterintuitive for persons who are used to strategic planning methods. Strategic planners start with possibilities to be considered and work to eliminate them, resulting in a single scenario to implement, complete with implementation steps, operating budgets, and action plans. Scenario-building is not designed to result in a single implementation scenario with accompanying business plan or budget. It is designed to flesh out possibilities for the many ways in which God could be working through the congregation; it is an act of imagination that helps people listen to God and, having listened, co-create with God. Scenario-builders bide their time, staying attuned with the congregation to signposts as God's purposes unfold.

This last step is not passive. The scenario-building group invites the entire congregation to participate in the adventure of this wilderness time, watching for signposts and reflecting theologically on what they see. The facilitator sets aside particular times when he or she asks questions such as how the congregation notes God's movement in the world during the week. Focus groups are established in churches with fifty or more members, where prayer and conversation center on God's movement in the local community and at national and international levels. Worship services include a time for discernment. Specialized studies, pertinent to the church's tradition, are held for the purpose of watching God's intent unfold in conversation and prayer.

This organic process may be uncomfortable for people who wish to take action soon after the scenarios are built. However, the facilitator and the scenario group can reassure the congregation that a wilderness time is necessary for discernment of God's movement. Six months to a year of theological reflection, watching, and grappling with questions would not be unusual. In this period, the following issues, among others, can be raised.

- Where is God moving? How is the future unfolding? Where is the energy in the congregation?
- How many random acts of kindness has the congregation noticed in the last week? What happened and who initiated them?
- Where do people notice God in the local community and in the national news?
- How does God relate to politics?
- What is the young adult population in the community doing? What are their concerns and how do they function in relationships? How does their activity relate to scenario possibilities?
- How does the local community connect together? What networks already are in place and what networks are forming? How is the church involved? Do social agencies and civic leaders welcome church-based input or is the church considered suspect in matters of charity and government?
- What are the interests of local benefactors?
- How does civic religion (popular, secularized Christianity) manifest itself in the community and in the nation? How does this manifestation affect the church?
- What is happening in the local business arena? What is happening in the world economic climate?
- How well are children being educated and what is the state of the school system? What kinds of education occur outside of school and church?
- What is the mood of the local clergy in terms of cooperative ventures?

Answers to these questions yield information about how the future is unfolding. Theological reflection by the church community on these topics is crucial at this point. Throughout the focused watching and reflection time, the overarching question is held before the congregation: What is God's movement and how does the congregation respond to it to co-create the future for the local church? Signposts become increasingly noticeable from the questions posed and through prayerful discernment. These clues begin to point to one or more scenarios. As a result, decisions about responding to God's movement in the church and world become increasingly clear because the scenario-builders have already been intentional about what responses are appropriate and possible to God's call. Refinement of scenarios occurs within the congregation and the church moves forward, meeting God's purpose as co-creators with God for wholeness and love. People of God find that they are moving into an ongoing, organic conversation, living in a posture of expectancy, watching for God's purpose as the future unfolds. The hope of moving through and out of the wilderness into new life comes alive particularly in this stage. Here inquiry no longer requires data gathering. It changes to mindfulness and centeredness, where evidence of God's purposeful work increasingly reveals itself.

Corner Church scenario-builders continue to share their work with the entire congregation, inviting everyone to pay attention to signposts or indications about what is evolving in front of them. To do so means living into possibilities as they emerge, noticing what might be the call for the adventure ahead. Does it look like Corner Church simply must close down? Is there a desire in the community to invest energy in revitalizing neighborhoods and addressing the needs of children and their families? Are there other churches interested in such a ministry? What is the mood of the local clergy? What is the mood of local authorities? What is the mood of the nation? Will the unchurched public be interested in an endeavor that may affect their own views of ministry? What inklings of God's movement are showing up in each of these areas? How many people in Corner Church notice these clues? These and other questions provide guidance for those watching and reflecting.

As God's purposes for future unfold, Corner Church is ready to co-create ministry with God. Members then live into the future, embracing hope through their present planning and continual flexibility. They notice God's call for them through ongoing theological and practical reflection about which futures are emerging. This living into possibility converts Corner Church to Process-Church.

To live into a time of active waiting and discernment, Corner Church will need to find ways to retain its investment in and focus on the process. Living in the wilderness of ambiguity based on hope for the future differs from the wilderness of despair and helplessness; nonetheless, taking time and developing discipline to discern is not easy. Rev. Jamie and the facilitator can develop plans for particular scripture studies that focus on the people of God in the wilderness or in exile, relating these stories to the story of Corner Church. Rev. Jamie also can orient worship to a discernment focus with attention to congregational stories about God's movement in the world during the week. An Advent theme suggests watching and waiting as a prayerful and liturgical discernment time for the community. Because Corner Church knows that its work is not meaningful without attention to God's purpose, members are open to the message of hope that they are important co-creators in God's unfolding future. Rev. Jamie has a significant role to play in order to keep this sense of adventure before the congregation. His own spiritual discipline and energy will need to focus on this work as he asks others to do the same. His role will help keep congregants' anxiety low, shifting the language of scarcity and depression to conversation about abundance and meaningful purpose. In this vital step, ever-evolving ministry in partnership with God emerges. Process-Church manifests itself in this way: the radical love of God connects with creation through constantly unfolding ministry opportunities for the people of Corner Church.

Implications of Scenario-building

Each of these scenario-building steps adds to the next in a process that moves the church from despair about decline or entrenchment in maintenance mode to an imaginative way to meet God in the present to co-create the future together. Theological work initially focuses congregations on the call for the church. Then the connection of emphases on discipline, focus, momentum and the concrete process for co-creating the future provides a means for the church to become process-oriented. In process orientation, the church finds relief from constant struggling for relevance as the world moves on. The Process-Church acknowledges its place in the wilderness by focusing on the opportunity found there to learn, watch, and become transformed into Christ's body perpetually claming new life. Wilderness becomes adventure in the midst of hardship, laced with hope instead of despair.

The implication of scenario-building is that there exists no end-point toward which participants are working; life and faith are a process, a journey. Scenario-building is one way in which the church evolves into its own future without abandoning its mainline connection. The discipline of staying in touch with context and working with it opens the door for churches to respond to both the local community and the world, while leading each into a new and better space at the same time. Rather than setting the church against the world or allowing the church simply to react to the world as many churches do, scenario-building creates opportunities for the church to be a significant and dynamic movement in the world. Process-Church offers alternative ways of addressing the challenge posed by the negative impacts of consumerism, globalized economics, and injustice. The church redefines success by answering a widespread, deeply felt yearning. The church is called to create a relevant yet radical message of wholeness and love for the local neighborhood and for the global family based in God's love.

REFLECTION QUESTIONS

1. Why are scenarios for the future important for the local faith community? What impact might they make?
2. How do understandings of globalization affect scenario-building? How does a group pay attention to postmodern persons' characteristic desires without relinquishing local church tradition completely? How is it possible for the church to be flexible in its worship and its understanding of mission?
3. How can scenario-building change the lives of the individuals participating? Is this change worthwhile in the long run? Is the commitment possible?

PART III

The Church in Transition

7

Living into Transition

What things tend to the service of God—keep us "Godward"?
That is the whole heart of the matter.

THOMAS MERTON[1]

Developing Process-Church as a way of understanding ecclesiology (the nature and mission of church) necessitates significant shifts in thinking and experience. Moving from church as a set, unchanging, unchallengeable institution to church as an open-ended movement requires an understanding of the emotional dynamics that will manifest themselves rapidly and widely during this shift. This chapter focuses specifically on the whole congregation's transition into living as Process-Church rather than the scenario-building group's work itself.

The challenge of creating Process-Church is to hold a foundational stability together with a transformational disequilibrium.[2] Imposition of structure, including a leadership structure as most programs and packages for church growth do, impedes living into Process-Church. A foundation for church does not depend on structures and goals established by church growth plans; it comes from the great commandment and is lived out in transformative ways. Therefore, an ethic of inquiry focused on biblical study, study of contexts, theological reflection, and scenario-building provides a means for eliciting the meaning of ministry based in the great commandment. This commandment provides a foundational structure (stability) for all transforming work that co-creates the future with God. At the same time, ongoing inquiry regarding the commandment's meaning in current context allows for constant reinterpretation about God's unfolding purposes (transformational disequilibrium).

Theological Transition

Living into transition begins with theological work that challenges widespread notions about the church. The long-term, modern model for being church retains Christian traditionalism, worships as faithful community, and invites non-Christians to be part of the theological and doctrinal claims about Truth. The church's foundation is understood to be a stable institution, established by followers of Christ, with unchangeable authority transmitted throughout the ages. Persons who accept the church's claim as possessor of eternal Truth can become members of the institution through baptism.

In contrast to this understanding of church, process thought claims that any entity must advance or die. "There is no standing still. The effort to repeat the past while holding the present at bay leads to decadence. The vitality and zest that were the essence of the worth of the past are lost."[3] Churches that defend their traditions without addressing the increasingly fast-paced technological advances, scientific breakthroughs, and cultural changes of the current era are rendered ineffective or invisible. However, if the church begins to understand its own nature as processive instead, it acknowledges its rich history, which adds weight to the present and future. Succession comes when believers in Jesus Christ claim their faith, reiterating this claim throughout history while interpreting faith for the present times.

> In this view, the church is not a stable, immutable institution that has existed since the time of Jesus, founded by him and protected by him from the changes of the world. The church is the consequence of its first members' faith in Jesus and the subsequent faith it inspired. In its dialogue with the world, that faith takes new shapes, thus giving new shapes to the church. In this sense, then, the church is constantly changing and readapting according to the exigencies of the world.[4]

Thus, change itself does not need merely to be tolerated, but to be embraced as the nature of the church's progress. Further, if the church is considered a living body of Christ that moves through history, building relationships and inviting others to faith, then its faith-relations are a creative force in society. As the spirit of Christ lives on in each faithful person, and each faithful person accumulates new experiences of faith, the church is always becoming rather than simply being. The church is first and foremost a process, an event moving through history,[5] rather than primarily a structure containing people who believe. "The definition of the church is always the people of the church in the act of creating the church."[6] The church contributes to society because its participants do. The varied expressions of faith add dynamism to the movement of church while it remains attentive to its tradition. Thus, as in process theory where the past shapes the present, which is lured into the future, tradition and dynamic change work together to unfold the future of the church.

Shifting attitudes about the nature and mission of the church introduce a paradox for church participants. It is clear that, in the Western world, individual freedoms and experiences are prized, even in the church. Private prayer and privatized faith in the midst of a community is a norm, manifesting itself in desire for personal salvation and personal relationship with Jesus. Process-Church adds the missing elements: connectedness with present community, with history, and with God's evolving future. This connectedness stretches back through time to the apostolic church and also links current church participants together. Process-Church cannot evolve without conversation about the community's mindfulness of God's work in the world, historically and presently. New capacities and connections emerge as individuals work out relationships. Systems of interdependence grow in complexity and connected people grow in relational skill. Paradoxically, Process-Church becomes both stable and dynamic in its connectedness with the past and with participants in the present, as it pays attention to the future.

> The individual holds the community in its awareness as the individual exercises its freedom to respond. When an individual changes, its neighbors take notice and decide how they will respond. Over time, individuals become so intermeshed in this process of coevolving that it becomes impossible to

distinguish the boundary between self and other, or self and environment. There is a continual exchange of information and energy between all neighbors, and a continuous process of change and adaptation everywhere in the system. And, in another paradox, these individual changes contribute to the overall health and stability of the entire system.[7]

While the theological work, conducted with appropriate focus and language and depth for the local context, may be convincing to some, the practical work of living into the future with an altered view of church is another matter. Moving from a limited view of church where the primary purpose is to dictate particular beliefs and norms, to a liberating view of church that calls persons to become the best possible creatures they can, takes time. The modernist notion that church should not be moved or influenced by anything external to itself does not come from any biblical injunction; this long-held understanding of church comes from the Greek idea that indifference to external forces is the ultimate strength.

On the other hand, church members are aware that certain theological beliefs such as creationism or biblical inerrancy no longer convince thoughtful people. Attempts to invite unchurched people to worship usually result in half-hearted responses or outright rejection. So local churches employ techniques in worship and programming that they think might appeal to the general public or particular target groups. However, when belief systems are challenged, churches have great difficulty questioning interpretations around which they have organized themselves for centuries. How can churches celebrate the tradition of Christianity as well as their particular traditions, and still be free enough to move into a future where new elements weave together with old to bring forth new possibilities? Being rooted in tradition does not necessarily mean that congregations cannot be open to the new; being open to the new does not necessarily betray tradition.

Churches have little trouble claiming that they are places of learning. Attendance at bible studies, desire for timely sermons that introduce authoritative perspectives on life's meanings, and conversation in small groups all imply that those who are present wish to learn. However, learning with any depth means that Christians must think critically about the destructive nature of some of their held beliefs. Tradition supports this premise. Justification for slavery, for example, is no longer considered appropriate despite biblical evidence that slavery was not challenged as a social institution in the early Christian movement.

Jesus himself called for change of beliefs without denying the roots of Judaism. His interpretation of law did not eliminate the law; it gave the law new life (Mt. 5:17–18). The great commandment itself is pushed further than its original interpretation: one must love one's enemies as well as one's neighbor, according to Luke's gospel (Lk. 6:27–28). Love exists for all people, for God is love and no one is excluded. To be in faithful relation to God, persons must not withhold love from neighbor or even enemy.

Because Christians are called to be lifelong learners and to live faithful, inspired lives, they are called to be critical thinkers about theological beliefs and understandings of the nature of church. Christians also are called to be critical thinkers about the society in which they live. Finally, they are called to embrace the work of God that occurs sometimes in spite of the church, particularly when the church has become entrenched in its practices and cannot see beyond itself. Indeed, faithful people who work outside the church for the wholeness of the world become more oriented toward risk-taking than people who preserve security in traditionalism. The opportunity to know the church's roots and to open the church to new ideas provides a creative tension from whence transformation is most likely to come.

Attitudes that already exist in churches regarding change of this magnitude will determine whether congregations are willing to work toward claiming new life. As described in chapter 2, Nancy Ammerman's study of congregations that are working for renewal concludes with the sense that these congregations are highly attuned to individual seekers' needs while at the same time attempting to create community where needs are addressed.[8] The distinction between trying to change and achieving change is important. For those congregations where little change occurred, Ammerman notes that either active resistance or lack of imagination precluded movement into a new understanding of the nature and mission of church in local context.[9]

Transition in the Wilderness

How does congregational attitude shift from fear-induced change to a sense of adventure about the church's future unfolding from a rich, textured tradition? How does the institutional church transition to Process-Church? The most important factor is that Process-Church does not define itself by a static typology. Church growth resources frequently define their ultimate goals by naming a type of church to which declining churches should aspire as an end-goal: emerging church, equipping church, discipling church, purpose-driven church, megachurch, metachurch, virtual church, deep church, and contemporary church, to name a few. The idea here is to instead create a sense of movement in congregations as they co-create their futures with God in particular ways, rather than providing lists for goal-oriented success. Success redefines itself in Process-Church on a continual basis as it meets God in the present and future, calling churches into an ever-evolving ministry. Transition work always starts with discovering which passions exist in congregations and how congregations make meaning.

Margaret Wheatley claims that organizational change and individual change come from the same place: "People need to explore an issue sufficiently as to whether new meaning is available and desirable. They will change only if they believe that a new insight, a new idea, or a new form helps them become more of who they are. If the work of change is at the level of an entire organization or community, then the search for new meaning must be done as a collective inquiry."[10]

In the case of local churches, inquiry of this nature begins transition through the preparatory stage in scenario-building. When congregations either experience dissonance with their current situations and/or have a genuine interest in thinking about their own level of faithfulness, they do not adapt to the cultures that the church is trying to attract. Instead, they critique their response to God's particular call. To discern this call based in the Great Commandment, groups think about what is most meaningful to them, individually and collectively. Rather than poring over mission or vision statements, people think through the meaning of radical love and how the nature of God is love played out in the world through Christ and through the church.

It is important to have a leader with some ability to aid the entire congregation in reflecting theologically on Jesus' great commandment as well as on current context. Frequently and consistently keeping the emphasis on how this commandment remains important for daily life before the congregation begins to create the ethos of inquiry. During transition, people pay close attention to each others' behaviors within the church and outside it; they formulate a reflective posture about the manifestations of love as they encounter them or initiate them daily. In addition, opportunities to sit in sacred space, *tenemos,* and time, *kairos,* together for intentional feedback about these observations generates energy for living into faith in a new way. Congregations now are working at a spiritual level as well as a theological level regarding their experience and understanding of faithful living. They are at the cusp of desiring new meaning, living into new life.

At this point, congregations understand that a group chosen from among them will enter the scenario-building process described in the last chapter. It is crucial that church members know that they are moving toward a time in the wilderness during this transition. Their self-assessment and subsequent discovery of deeper spiritual connections in relationship and new understandings of the great commandment yield excitement at the journey's outset. Creative ideas for ministry follow alongside the scenario-building work, perhaps with some short-term implementation that channels the high energy level. People become more motivated and focused, anticipating meaning as co-creating the future with God. They are invited to give input to the scenario-building group, providing ideas and information for the group's work.

However, this newfound zeal is not shared by everyone within the congregation and even fewer of those outside of it. Energy begins to wane and disillusionment about the impact of the initial response to reflection on the great commandment sets in. People have arrived at the edge of the wilderness. The penchant for immediate results, namely higher attendance in worship, attraction of the unchurched, or the much-hoped-for impact upon areas of injustice has been challenged. Now what? If there is no sign of a next step, anxiety rises and congregations return to their original sense of ill-being and resulting depression.

So it is important for leaders to describe the wilderness, assuring congregations that claiming new life will mean spending some time in that wilderness, where results are not quick, and a promised land does not seem to be in sight. Some may wish to abandon the journey at this point because the wilderness seems similar to the stagnant state they have experienced already. Others need to be reassured that any significant change of ethos requires this stage; the challenge of living in the wilderness together is crucial for new life.

Wilderness is not dead space and time. Much can happen in it. The wilderness may feel chaotic to some people. However, assurances that chaos can lead to reorganization in new ways, providing unforeseen vision for a promised land, can help people survive the wilderness time.

Gilbert Rendle, in *Leading Change in the Congregation,* describes this wilderness phenomenon, naming it as an essential part of a chaotic model of change. "A chaotic model begins with an understanding of change that recognizes the reality and value of a time of chaos (messiness, lack of clarity, a need for wandering)."[11] When people become sensitive to what is incomplete or missing in their faith and in their church and then risk new ways of thinking and behaving in terms of their faith, they are delivered into chaos, according to Rendle.[12] He quotes John Scherer on the role of chaos:

> For transformation to occur, the existing mental box must fall away like the discarded skin on a molting snake. The operating pattern must be broken down. We must find ourselves released from the grip of the old context. This leaves us, not immediately with a new pattern, but with empty space with which a new pattern (creation) can occur. In other words, we must find ourselves in a chaotic void, without any life jacket or props or ideas about how to proceed, with nothing to hold on to, no way to save ourselves. In that instant, we are open to what could show up, which could not have shown up as long as we were holding on to anything we thought would save us from the experience of being in an empty space.[13]

If congregants understand that wilderness invites chaos, required for substantive change from habitual institutional thinking to process thought, then they have the opportunity to fend off their desire to change back to the old ways to alleviate discomfort in the wilderness. It is therefore important to connect the congregation intentionally to biblical narratives of wilderness struggle and deliverance. Creativity comes from chaos, as shown in the Genesis story; the promised land comes from wandering in the wilderness, as shown in the exodus story. Without this time and discomfort faced by the people of God, lasting change would not have occurred.

Study of chaos informs what can happen in the wilderness, showing people the potential for transformation, thereby lowering anxiety. Physics gives insight: energy created in and through chaos enables transformation of subatomic particles, analogous to systems of behavior affecting human beings. As process thought relies on principles of science from Whitehead's studies,[14] so does chaos theory:

> When a system is held in chaos long enough, the system approaches the threshold of substantive change that could not be reached in any other fashion. This is one of the central learnings of the new physics, which works at the subatomic level. It was discovered that a molecule held in chaos can be brought to a condition of excitement and self-regulation that will allow it to reorganize at a higher level.[15]

Further, everything is interrelated in a system, leaving nothing unaffected. In times of chaos, the system itself moves from equilibrium to high energy, affecting change. In physics, the environment and the system interact. In the church the same phenomenon occurs as people and their environments connect, moving to new ways of thinking and organizing. Margaret Wheatley says, "In describing self-organization, I am always struck by the great partnering that exists between the system and its environment. As the system changes and evolves, it also affects its environment. No participant in the dance is left unaffected by changes that occur in the other."[16]

Human beings do not need to fear disequilibrium, according to Wheatley. There is a path through change that leads to greater resilience.[17] Self-renewal and self-transcendence result from systems that remain in chaos long enough to be lured into new possibilities of creation. There is a choice for human beings in the midst of a wilderness that seems like chaos: living in panic or depression, causing people to move back to the old ways, or opening up to new adventures and anticipation of new life.

Generating a sense of adventure in the wilderness experience in spite of the feeling of chaos will help people enter it more readily.

The scenario-building group can continue to share its work with the congregation at this time, providing evidence that there is movement in the wilderness and requesting prayerful support and input. Worship and prayer focus on the journey at this juncture, providing hope and courage. The wilderness experience has potential to set people free because they see the possibilities of new beginnings.

Thinking about the long-term picture of this journey will provide further reassurance for wilderness times. Perceiving the long view leads people from the current sense of spiritual and economic decline to the hope of entering a new process of continual learning and living in love. The discipline of seeing the whole as interrelationships and patterns of change provides a means by which people survive the barren spaces.[18]

Process thought is integral to this discipline because it requires persons to shift from seeing increments of time and experience as independent from each other. It also challenges the understanding of people as helpless reactors to the present by seeing a large picture of the future, where human beings are part of the future's co-creation.[19] Congregants have already begun to think in terms of interrelationships based on human connection with God and each other through their reflection on the great commandment. Continued focus on interrelationship helps to make the wilderness experience transformative in and of itself, while moving toward a transformed future.

The outcome of such a wilderness experience for a congregation or the scenario-building group itself eludes definition. Linear "if... then" statements are not the final answer in this process of becoming; they simply provide a framework for the journey. There remains a foundational congruity based in the great commandment even though no final end point can be determined other than whether a congregation lives in process or not. Churches that walk in the wilderness may find themselves evolving in ways that look completely different than other churches. They seem unique to the onlooker. The list of types of churches will not matter to these congregations; they do not aspire to be like anyone else. They aspire to be faithful to their call and to fulfill the great commandment in the best way possible for their context.

Emotional Transition

A shift in perspective about the nature and mission of the church requires attention not only to the functional transition but to the emotional transition as well. Rendle describes the emotional cycle for congregations who experience change.[20] People begin with excitement when a new discovery is made or a new plan of action is introduced, perhaps entertaining positive outcomes initially. Given time to think about change, however, people naturally begin to feel unsettled or uneasy. They have choices about how they work with their uneasiness, but if they are assured that this reaction is normal, they may choose to live with their discomfort. However, if the discomfort seems unacceptable to them, then resistance grows, perhaps to the point of denial. Resistance and denial are means of self-protection because fear has become acute.

Feelings of living in chaos often discovered in the wilderness eventually may take the form of grief. It is in the wilderness where people grieve over what they are giving up. They are being asked to release their notions of the glory days that they hoped they could recover, as well as their long-held theological assumptions, their stereotypes of successful churches, and their habits of searching for the quick-fix to make them successful.

Reassurance from a calm leader about the value of letting go is crucial at this stage; releasing what is familiar is the most difficult act in the change process and is accompanied by low energy and perhaps depression. Some people stay with the wilderness process and others decide to leave at this point. Still others remain "stuck" at this stage and decline to continue participating actively in the congregation but remain in attendance.

Rendle then observes that people staying with the transition begin to reorganize, welcoming new possibilities for the future. Congregations can imagine playing out new scenarios. People show propensities to take risks. They acknowledge that failure resulting from risk-taking is possible, but not limiting. For example, if congregants ask how they are to love neighbor in the local context and also while connecting with the wider world, they might find that their vision for ministry looks radically different than it ever has. They may sell their church building altogether or they may network town agencies with churches. They may travel or stay at home. They may walk the streets with the homeless or they may start a faith in the workplace opportunity. It is here, in this stage, that the hope for the future comes alive. People begin to embrace their futures based on what they know about their context and their commitment to their calls. They commit to meeting God so that the future opens up, co-creating with God the possibility for ministry based in God's purposes.[21]

The final stage is what Rendle describes as "integrating the change."[22] The congregation chooses to live into the new behavior or process. People make decisions that include theological reflection and well-informed, well-paced processes of discernment. They live as process-oriented people rather than solution-based people. Living into an unfolding future calls for celebration of a church continually reinventing itself, the Process-Church. Congregations find that they have created new identities and structures based on sharing the good news of the gospel with conviction and love.

Transition and Conflict

Conflicted congregations present a different challenge. And indeed, one can observe that most mainline congregations are conflicted at some level. Loren Mead of the Alban Institute paints such a picture:

> Our congregations, whatever else they are, are seething pools of conflict. We have different ways of decorating altars and we fight about it. We have different ideas about who the pastor should be, and we fight about it. Sometimes our fights are donnybrooks, but more often they are the tight-lipped, controlled, hard-to-finish type. The grudge-generating kind. Some fights turn into feuds that last generations. Sometimes those outside congregations are more comfortable than we in dealing with differences. We "religious" folk have a way of calling God in to the fight to help us destroy the opposition.[23]

Hostility precludes the desire to live into the process of co-creating the future with God. Indeed, hostility focuses on itself, eliminating love's movement toward God and neighbor. Instead, it escalates negative emotional energy or shuts down energy altogether.

Each emotional system found in a congregation affects all the others; when the emotional system functions poorly, work, communication, and decision-making systems also function poorly.[24] Communication in churches that live in a long-term, conflicted atmosphere tends to inhibit any desire for adventure. Rather, in these toxic situations, communication focuses on power differentials rather than healthy relationships. Attempts to resolve conflict in long-term toxic situations are met with escalated resistance.

Conflict theory indicates that in situations of chronic conflict, what seems like chaos is really organized patterns of behavior. People who do not speak to each other for years still remain connected by their tension; the pattern is not to speak. If one party chooses to change behavior and speak, the system of emotional fields changes. In these moments, where an incremental shift in a system occurs, potential for new energy arises. The other party has a choice. He or she can push the first party to change back by not speaking in response, or he or she can respond in some fashion. The choice at this juncture determines whether change is possible or if the emotional system will be maintained as it has been. If change occurs based on the decisions of the participants in the system, actual chaos sets in as patterns are broken and people attempt to find a new equilibrium.

Effective management of unresolved or irresolvable conflict by a non-anxious leader allows the church to move forward on occasion, particularly when an opening occurs where creativity can break through. Any creativity will change the emotional system. At another level, conflict understood as an opportunity for transformation of relationships requires a willingness on the part of the participants in the emotional system to want to change. People discover inklings of wholeness when they work through the toxicity of their behaviors with each other. They may even learn how to use conflict for growth as they face issues of power and fear. Descriptions of how to promote such changes are well documented in systems and conflict literature.[25]

Only when conflicted churches desire to do the internal work required to change their own emotional systems will there be potential for moving into an ethic of inquiry. Energy focused on maintaining personal power or living in fear leaves little momentum for thinking about the call of the faith community and its co-creating potential. Unless toxic conflict can be shifted into pursuit of common hopes and dreams for the church, the emotional systems of the church will preclude claiming new life. The local congregation itself will need to determine if it is willing to undertake the hard work of working through conflict before scenario development for the future can begin. Without common desire to move forward, development of Process-Church will not occur.

Transition and Relevance

Thus far, we have focused on internal church dynamics. However, internal systems do not function independently of the external systems surrounding churches. Postmodern attitudes, globalizing forces, and the perceived irrelevance of the mainline church contribute to the challenges congregations face as they think about claiming new life. Transition requires significant attention to these forces without allowing them to dictate the role of the church. Falling into the trap of becoming relevant to the world for relevancy's sake is one danger of the transitional journey.

Mainline churches experience anxiety over standards of success adopted from the business world. There is pressure to increase income and human resources, termed "assets" in an increasing number of church redevelopment programs.[26] This definition of success tempts churches to be relevant in the "market" of the outside world. Adaptation to external cultures makes sense when congregations do so to live out their calls more effectively than they can by ignoring these cultures. However, a problem arises when this desire to be relevant leads congregations to uncritical adaptation; relevance collapses into uncritical surrender to worldly standards of success.

Os Guinness, a social scientist and writer, discusses this surrender through four stances that people take when they succumb to anxiety.[27] First, people make assumptions that the globalizing, economic worldviews or postmodern trends are significant enough to be superior to what Christians know, so they adopt these worldviews as part of Christian thought practice without critical analysis. He uses capitalism as an illustration of this uncritical adoption:

> For instance, modern capitalism is clearly the most powerful engine in all history for creating wealth, but that does not mean that we should adopt all the principles of market

capitalism without critiquing them. Assumptions about anything, whether capitalism, science, politics, psychology, patriotism, fast food, or the place of celebrities in modern society, should all be recognized and carefully examined.[28]

Second, Guinness claims that everything that does not fit into new fads or trends is neglected or abandoned without assessment. "Is the traditional idea unfashionable, superfluous, or just plain wrong? No matter. It doesn't fit in, so it has to go."[29] If the idea is not new and glamorous, it has no economic value, so there is no need to include it in one's thinking. Standards set by the marketplace then become accepted without challenge.

Third, anything of tradition that remains is altered to fit the new assumption of value set by the world. For example, the capitalist value signifying that "time equals money" diminishes the desire to spend time volunteering rather than writing checks to support ministries. Or consider how people enjoy having choices when they shop. So churches provide a smorgasbord of programming options from which congregants can choose. The assumption about the value itself becomes authoritative and tradition is adapted to it. Adaptability itself is not problematic, because cross-cultural beliefs and practices can inform internal cultures in life-giving, creative ways. The key to adaptation is that it is constructive and intentional rather than merely adopted without thought.[30]

Finally, Guinness calls the culmination of the first three factors "assimilation." Assimilation to the secular culture ultimately leads to capitulation. This capitulation can lead to rapid change, but, in the midst, the church loses its center. To continue with the example introduced above: when time equals money and church members write checks to support ministries rather than volunteering, they have no personal involvement with neighbors or strangers. As a result, they have little connection with persons outside their families and friends and therefore have no idea about how to live out the great commandment. This disconnection with the foundational center of faith further promotes anxious reliance on fads or trends to renew congregations. Anxiety-based change does not lead to transformation; it simply attempts to fill the sanctuary seats by being relevant to the latest target audience:

Some have spent the last decades reinventing churches furiously according to the dictates of the baby boomers. Others are now pronouncing that passé and are tackling the task with the same enthusiasm to court the younger generation. But what links them all is the same principle. The authentic church is the relevant church, and the relevant church is the attuned church, and the attuned church is the church in sync with its audience.[31]

Guinness lists the losses as churches succumb to market temptations: loss of courage, loss of continuity with tradition, loss of credibility in terms of believable substance, and loss of identity.[32] When churches yield to the temptation to capitulate to culture rather than being versatile with it through flexibility and challenge, they lose sight of God's call to transformational work for wholeness and love.[33]

Change rarely is easy. Inviting a church to think about itself differently so that it can fulfill its call faithfully is complicated and difficult work. Factors that impede this transition remain strong; congregants' fear of wilderness that includes chaos, inability to predict the future, temptation to find easy ways to "fix" the church, low energy, little passion, and disconnection from God's call all contribute to resistance. A patient, persistent leader who does not fear conflict or change and who can live with ambiguity is essential for this transition from institutional church to Process-Church.

REFLECTION QUESTIONS _____

1. What are the barriers to transition in the local church? What is the importance of comfort derived from routine and habit? What is the importance of change?
2. How does chaos become opportunity? What are the dangers of the wilderness? What are the blessings?
3. How does transition affect anxiety? How does anxiety affect transition? What kinds of conversation can make a difference regarding the emotional aspects of change?

8

Leadership and Process-Church

*I am convinced that those who will give leadership to a
renewed and renewing church are those who will dare to
experience both pain and possibility, then challenge the
church to risk the same. This is a time of crisis, of danger and
opportunity.*

HOWARD E. FRIEND[1]

Intelligent, flexible leaders initiating transition to Process-Church
are crucial for calling and organizing a church to live in a new way.
Hundreds of secular leadership books on bookstore shelves tell the
public "how to" lead and what skills are necessary for success, whether
it be financial, managerial, or chief executive-oriented success. One
may be tempted to delve into such books to find the formulae that
leaders use to promote personal skill sets and apply these formulae
to Process-Church.[2] This chapter introduces a different way of
approaching the leadership necessary for the church's transformation.
Situating leaders within the call of the great commandment grounds
them in a foundation different than acquiring skill sets for success.

Success for leaders typically is defined as profitable results or
outcomes in their organizations, quality of relationships with followers,
or survival in difficult organizational cultures. When grounded in the
commandment to love God and neighbor, leaders have a different
notion of success. Leadership is not leadership for its own sake, but

for the sake of others developing their own potentials and making meaning in the world yearning for connection and purpose.

Leadership Challenges

Process-Church leaders who have an eye for transformational change recognize their need to understand helpful and harmful global influences on local church contexts. Positive aspects of new technologies not only widen communication networks but they also provide means by which economic and political events are monitored and interpreted all over the world. Communications provide idea-sharing with someone on the other side of the globe and the ability to be available or provide aid to someone in need within minutes.[3]

Immediacy stemming from high-tech communications has its own pressures for leaders. They receive information and requests from multiple sources and are expected to respond just as quickly. Few leaders who endure busy schedules have time to reflect theologically on their own church responsibilities or on the complex systems that affect their church's work. Fast-paced living becomes habit. Likewise, as leaders introduce Process-Church ideas, they can be tempted to react quickly to stem growing anxiety about unresolved issues, particularly if they are leaders in declining churches. If leaders resist the temptation to react, they will afford themselves deeper, more meaningful responses, informed by the input of other leaders and followers. They will remain non-anxious, modeling this demeanor for those whose anxiety rises at the thought of transition.

Leaders of Process-Churches also will understand that in order to create a culture in which change can start anywhere within the church, they must establish an environment of teamwork and mutual trust. Trust takes years to build. It requires meeting people where they are before inviting them to move to a new place. In the midst of trust-building, leaders have to be careful about their own ego-needs and boundaries by embracing honest self-awareness.

Too many leaders protect ego by justifying their own visions for the church as the correct vision because they are trained professionals or have a "parent knows best" attitude. Some churches expect this type of authoritarian leadership from a paid professional. These congregations tend not to be motivated for lay-empowered ministry. In other churches, the fallout of such leadership approaches leads to unhealthy conflict, with blame and shame controlling conversations. Even those leaders who employ consultants to "fix" the problem of lay attitudes often find that they remain "correct" about the vision but have lost the support of the people with whom they are trying to be in ministry.

Leaders who believe that they will have control over predictable situations in the church will be disappointed quickly. "Individuals and organizations operate with spontaneity and unpredictability. Effective leaders foster a tolerance for uncertainty, even chaos."[4] Leaders who can live with the tensions of ambiguity and uncertainty often are capable of waiting for a deeper meaning to emerge:

> To be a leader is to live in the middle—in the tension between a future vision and the current reality. This tension is inherent if a leader becomes the steward of God's vision for the congregation. One cannot give in to the current reality and abandon the vision to which God is calling the church. Nor can one simply lift up the vision and ignore the realities. To be a leader means to stay with the tension. It also means to stay with the people.[5]

This ability, carried out with loyalty and fortitude, is exactly what people are seeking.

Unfortunately, some leaders desire to be professional ministers because they are looking for a community to support them and provide reinforcement for their own need to be loved. This motive for entering church leadership, often disguised in the language of vocational call, results ultimately in disillusionment, anger, and burnout for such leaders and for the community. These leaders constantly try to reestablish themselves in new settings, only to find that the pattern repeats itself within two or three years. Because leaders themselves often do not recognize their own complicity in the repetition of poor performance, they perpetuate anxiety in an increasingly wider network of churches unless they are released from ministry duties.

However, if one considers systems theory, the understanding that quality of relational connection determines the health of an organization, then one cannot pinpoint the leader alone as the cause for churches failing to be in ministry. Tense environments, fear of closure, a history of conflict, or a desire to remain in the status quo for the sake of perceived safety are all factors that affect the leadership context. It takes self-differentiated, mature leadership to create enough safe space so that assumptions, fears, and habits can be addressed honestly before the work of collaborative inquiry begins. So, if leaders have primarily self-interested motives for entering ministry and they encounter faith communities that are protecting their own self-interests, there will be no room to move forward into meaningful ministry together. Each self-interested party will simply end up attempting to "win" power for its own interest, whether it be creating a successful megachurch or preserving tradition even unto death.

Thus, leaders' characters and motives in faith communities struggling to become faithful followers of God are crucial to the larger conversation about the transformation of the church for the sake of the world. Leaders who do not fear conflict but instead understand conflict as opportunity for change, who have a sense of humor and who have the spiritual fortitude to keep hope alive for the future will be essential for the development of the Process-Church.

Ethic of Inquiry for Leaders

Leaders begin their own spiritual, emotional, and intellectual work before they introduce process thinking to the congregations. They open themselves to inquiry and transformation through their own desire to become vulnerable and learn. To do so, they attend to an interplay of intuition, thought, and action.[6] The essence of this kind of leadership is itself process-oriented, whereby leaders remain open to new revelations on a continuing basis. Management theories and skill development alone do not function at this level; this type of leader lives in the balance of his or her own attention and the external world simultaneously. A process-oriented leader listens to the impact of tradition from the past radiating into the future at the inclusive present moment.[7] Bill Torbert, Professor of Management at Boston College, describes them as people of "reframing mind and spirit."

A reframing spirit continually overcomes itself, awakening to its own presuppositions. A reframing mind continually listens into the dark of preverbal experience. It adjusts itself to the frames of reference held by other actors in a situation, to underlying organizational and historical developmental rhythms, and to the as yet unorganized chaos beyond. (As we now theoretically know, unorganized chaos represents by far the larger part of reality at any moment, yet is largely inaccessible to the language and assumption-bound mind.)[8]

Listening at this level is an active silence, a listening into silence that co-creates a sense of being, knowing, receiving, and doing.

Leaders of this ilk also learn to stand in the middle of apparent opposites, or paradoxes, seeking to blend them by reframing the issues at hand. In this way, they help the powerless, or those who feel powerless, generate a sense of power that can create change. This power is relational rather than a commodity that can be possessed. This power is also meant to increase awareness and alertness, learning, a sense of mutuality, and participation in transformation.[9]

One example of how power of this nature can be released is when the leader can reflect on intentional life-immersion experiences and then invites others into these experiences. The leader helps participants reframe their lenses by asking provocative questions about their perspectives. Invited to immerse themselves in different socioeconomic cultures, participants may reflect that they are amazed at the hope some destitute people feel, despite living in horrific conditions. Many participants who have not experienced such conditions do not understand this hope. They simply marvel and do not engage in the work of reflection about the nature of hope in the midst of despair or how hope manifests itself in their own contexts. Paulo Freire, author of *Pedagogy of the Oppressed*, describes this phenomenon:

> When people lack a critical understanding of their reality, apprehending it in fragments which they do not perceive as interacting constituent elements of the whole, they cannot truly know that reality. To truly know it, they would have to reverse their starting point: they would need to have a total vision of the context in order subsequently to separate and isolate its constituent elements and by means of this analysis achieve a clearer perception of the whole.[10]

The leader who has adopted an ethic of inquiry utilizes this situation to guide participants through theological and sociopolitical reflection. The leader also encourages listening of the deepest kind.

A specific example describing how a leader can invite participants' critical understanding of their immersion context might be to raise consciousness about American history of slavery. Hope for slaves was generated through song that lifted up the belief that afterlife would bring relief, freedom, and wholeness. The leader invites participants to deeper inquiry: hope in the afterlife also kept many slaves in captivity on earth. With this realization on the part of participants, leaders can formulate observations and questions regarding paradox: distant hope for slaves became a tool of oppression as well as a tool of survival, depending on one's social location. This simple yet not necessarily obvious observation introduces a clearer perception of the whole context as Freire describes.

Continued inquiry facilitated by the leader finally brings participants back to the context in which they currently are immersed. Participants have a deeper perspective on both oppression and survival and can begin to question how this context came to be in the first place. The potential in this example is for the privileged to understand the call of their privileged position, which is to love neighbor by opening doors so that oppressed peoples may walk through in this day and age.

This approach underscores the need for leadership to understand global and local contexts and the work of the church in the margins. Implicit in this inquiry process is the foundational great commandment. The motive behind inquiry in groups where leaders practice theological reflection themselves remains the same: persons are called to love God and love neighbor as self. Flexibility and ability to ask questions that are both prophetic and pastoral are crucial characteristics of such leaders. These leaders ground themselves by answering the call to bring about God's purpose of love; then they call the church community to do likewise.

How do leaders develop their mindsets and spiritual centering for a personal ethic of inquiry? Initially leaders experience a sense of their own discontent with the status quo. The actions and policies of many corporations and Western governments perpetuate socioeconomic difficulty for the vast majority of the world. Leaders must respond on the basis of the meaning of the great commandment. Dissatisfaction and even pain regarding the ineffectiveness of the church in the midst of growing economic gaps, environmental crises, and health pandemics pull people into a desire to be in leadership in ways that have not been defined entirely to date. These persons who desire change and are looking for a means to participate in change are the very leaders who are most ready to enter the world of inquiry and Process-Church. They are also the people who will undertake the difficult task of inviting the church to exist differently than it has for centuries. They are explorers, ready for a new path while being faithful to the best legacies of Christianity throughout the ages.

Those who feel called to Process-Church leadership may employ a variety of approaches to develop a ministry of inquiry based on the great commandment. First, forming collegial groups for theological reflection on ministry in various contexts will be a crucial ongoing spiritual formation venue for leaders. One does not lead in isolation; one also does not learn in isolation. These peer groups engage in the very process outlined in previous chapters, including scenario-building for the future of leadership in the post-Christendom church. Combining experiences of ministry and study of both local and global contexts, peers begin to develop imaginative leadership possibilities. They also engage in conversation that concretely outlines the invitation to local congregations to begin to move into an ethic of inquiry based on principles of faith. Creating scenarios for the future involves the homework of reflecting on power structures locally and globally while fostering the ability to reflect theologically on the impact of these structures on people's lives.

Second, leaders developing a personal ethic of inquiry consult the body of wisdom that has surfaced through leadership experience in the church and in other fields. Leaders who focus on changing cultures in secular and ecclesial organizations also rely heavily on informed intuition rather than on mere reaction to data. Spiritual texts offer another resource for leadership formation, again best reflected upon in a group setting for a variety of perspectives. Resources that move beyond simple skill-based teaching and repeatedly elevate the importance of self-awareness, context-awareness, and the ability to listen well provide the most valuable insight for the leadership task at hand.[11]

Leaders face challenges when inviting congregations to seek new life. By giving up their own behaviors and unexamined belief systems that have not led to faithful responses to God's call, they model possibilities for change for the church. Motives focusing on people's potentials, openness to inquiry, and investment in process thought all are prerequisites for the leadership work required to develop Process-Church. Most of all, leaders must desire to co-create the future with God, just as they hope that the congregation will partner in doing so with them.

REFLECTION QUESTIONS

1. How does a leader's own ethic of inquiry affect the church? How does a leader challenge him or herself?
2. What particular leadership skills aid leaders as they turn toward a process orientation? Are these same skills necessary for followers in a Process-Church?
3. How do leaders name their own definitions of success in light of the great commandment? How does a leader articulate call with regard to Process-Church leadership?

PART IV

The Churches

9

The Process-Church
Four Narratives

*As we create communities from the cohering center of shared
significance, from a mutual belief in why we belong together,
we will discover what is already visible everywhere around us
in living systems. Our great creativity and diversity, our desire
for contribution and relationships, blossom when the heart of
our community is clear and beckoning, and when we refrain
from cluttering our paths with proscriptions and demands. The
future of community is best taught to us by life.*

MARGARET WHEATLEY[1]

Established congregations who face challenges regarding their
futures often have spent time and energy trying to reverse decline,
often to no avail. Despite attempts to reverse waning financial giving
and attendance, many congregations find that they remain concerned
about their viability as churches. The ethic of inquiry is unlikely to be a
part of these congregations' lives in their current states. By introducing
an ethic of inquiry to the mainline church with a new focus, leaders
can invite churches to live into their potentials.

Creating scenarios as outlined in chapter 6 is one means by which the ethic of inquiry begins to come to the fore as an ethos. Scenarios require participants to conduct research about their context, to name and challenge implicit understandings of their own social location within their context, and to spur imagination about the future.[2] Building scenarios not only provides faith communities ways to respond to the unfolding present-future continuum, it also disarms anxiety and desire for quick-fix solutions. Once congregations begin to embrace thoughtful theological and contextual reflection and free themselves to be imaginative, the process takes hold and becomes a new way of claiming life. The future looks less frightening and challenges become adventures.

There are limits to scenarios. They provide a means for congregations to look at potential futures imaginatively and realistically. Scenario-building, however, does not address directly internal institutional conflicts, dysfunction, staff or lay-clergy dynamics, or immediate crises. Yet these issues either ease as congregations begin to find a long-term hope toward which they can work together, or become clearer so that churches can work on conflict or crisis before moving into scenario-building.

The four narratives that follow further illustrate the process set forth in this book, indicating the challenges that congregations face and what might happen if they were to employ the ethic of inquiry, complete with scenario-building, in their particular contexts. Each church described here is experiencing decline in some form despite opportunities, and, in two cases, attempts to change. Names and locations have been changed to honor congregations' anonymity; general descriptions of each setting therefore can provide prototypes for many congregations.[3] Examples of an inquiry process, including scenario-building exercises, follow each description of a church setting, illustrating the methodology for moving to Process-Church as a new way of being church.

Components of the preparatory work differ in each case because they account for differing contexts and mindsets of participants. Nonetheless, the ethic of inquiry and scenario-building process remain centered on genuine options and real choices in each case. University Church follows a step-by-step outline to illustrate the process clearly. Remaining examples consist of a more fluid narrative format.

University Church

University Church has been well established since its inception in the late 1880s. The stone building is a small version of Chartres Cathedral, with soaring stained glass windows and a commanding pipe organ situated in the balcony of the sanctuary. At capacity, the church sanctuary holds five hundred people. The church stands in a busy urban, middle-class neighborhood, in the shadow of a world-renowned university with 20,000 students in attendance. Two blocks away, a major shopping and entertainment area, patronized by city residents, students, and faculty alike, teems with crowds day and night. University Church itself is not visible from the shopping area without some effort; it is surrounded by multi-level apartments and homes. There is no parking available other than for staff; those attending services, meetings, or programs must walk, take public transportation, or park on the considerably over-crowded streets.

University Church formally claims the university as part of its parish. Thus, the minister, Rev. Clare, is called upon to lead university chapel services when the chaplain is not available. University events requiring a parish minister include Rev. Clare. University Church members remain proud of their connection to the local university and desire to include professors and students in their own worship services.

The denomination in which University Church resides has four other churches in the university area, all experiencing membership decline. Each of the five churches maintains a large stone building that needs hundreds of thousands of dollars in repair and continuous upkeep. There has been conversation in the denomination about closing one church and sharing three ministers among the remaining four congregations within the next decade. The five churches have met to discuss an initial proposal based on parish demographics and church trends, but little action has resulted. The churches realize that, despite proximity and attempts to introduce programs for the university students, little or no response contributes to their congregational decline.

University Church understands itself as a "remnant" community, with forty to sixty members in worship on Sundays. All members are Caucasian. On Sundays, members sit in small groups of two and three throughout the large space, greeting each other politely before and after the worship service. Congregational singing usually has been drowned out by the pipe organ, but the organ is no longer is working condition; there are no funds for repair. Hymns are accompanied by a small piano at this point.

Pride in the history of the church and also in the faded glory of the building bolsters church members each Sunday, causing them to ignore the rate of decline that will shut their doors within two to three years. Rev. Clare has spent seven years working with congregational leaders to develop a new vision for ministry together with other local congregations of the denomination. She notes members blocking change whenever new ideas arise. The church's focus remains inward and its financial giving is diminishing in the midst of growing needs in the city. Rev. Clare herself works with the poor through a mission program adopted by the denomination in the area, but sees little response from the congregation to the program other than occasional, minimal financial support. Rev. Clare intends to apply for a position in another parish within the year.

The unique ministry at University Church is its commitment to worship and biblical discussion. Members invite speakers on occasion to present ideas and facilitate discussion in conjunction with an evening worship service. Intellectual discourse about current topics fits the profile of the membership consisting of retired university faculty and staff, professionals, and business leaders. Focus on intellectual endeavor and biblical study remain part of the internal culture at University Church; other than invited speakers and worship leaders, there is little connection with the surrounding community and even less desire to pursue new participation in the life of the church.

An Ethic of Inquiry for University Church

Theological Reflection

Theological reflection on the state of University Church's ministry provides perspective on members' understanding of their faith and resulting actions. Reflection in University Church's case opens opportunity for self-assessment in terms of focus on ministry endeavors rather than sustaining an intellectual enclave. Further, naming how members consciously articulate their faith and how they live into it allows University Church to critique its current understanding of the mission and purpose of church. If members are willing to undertake this challenge to reflect on ministry, they might discover possibilities that fit their membership profile and begin to move them into a new way of becoming church.

When is a church not a church? Simply participating in liturgies and intellectual conversation does not fulfill the understanding of *koinonia,* which Christians understand as the fellowship of the Holy Spirit (2 Cor. 13:14). University Church expresses its belief system through its attendance at worship services and study sessions, thereby relying heavily on intellectualism and loyalty to the local church as primary components for faithful living. In fact, theological reflection itself might be a welcome exercise for members who have a broad knowledge of theological thinkers. Responding to their own faith systems in daily living as a result of reflection poses a different kind of challenge for them.

The self-proclaimed "remnant" is inward-focused and has no vision for the future of University Church. Members seem to be in denial. Ignoring the situation in which University Church finds itself has led to intellectual exercise and legalism. Denial of the church's unpleasant reality coupled with the avoidance of God's movement closes the door to God's possibility for the future and keeps University Church circling in the wilderness without hope. If there is no openness to conversion or imagination, there can be no transformation or new life. God, in divine grace, will continue to invite this congregation to choose life, but the choice is theirs.

Evidence of Jesus' interpretation of the commandment to love is not visible at University Church. Perhaps love of God is acknowledged privately, but there is no way of knowing. Communal life, *koinonia,* does not yield public conversation about faith or development of faith practices as a community aside from prescribed worship led by clergy. University Church members do not engage with others inside or outside the church in conversations about or in acts of ministry. Small groups of friends care for each other and sit together on Sundays, though not within a context of *koinonia.* As a result of this privatized religion, no outward manifestation of love of neighbor exists for the community. The dryness of the wilderness becomes clear; there is no passion for the faith journey. University Church will need to decide if it wishes to begin to walk through the wilderness toward living waters.

Admission of thirst can be addressed only when people give up self-sufficiency. Indeed, if pride prevents persons from desiring water, and therefore they never turn toward the well, then they become dehydrated and die, often exclaiming that they do not deserve what has befallen them. The exodus story speaks to such a situation: Why doesn't God rescue God's people from the wilderness immediately? The people of God had hardened their hearts, preferring familiar surroundings and death to walking through the wilderness and hardship into new life (Ex. 16:2–3).

University Church sits in the midst of a globalizing local community. Neighborhoods surrounding the church house multicultural groups, with different religions represented from apartment to apartment and house to house. One foray into the main shopping area results in exposure to at least five languages spoken at any given time. The university itself has a significant name in the world scientific community and is technologically advanced. Students of the arts and humanities also contribute to the university's good reputation and provide opportunities for the public to experience creative arts. Food, clothing, and specialty shops cater to a diverse clientele with highly educated and world-savvy tastes.

Add to this global-local context[4] the notion of the post-Christendom church. The chapel at the university is used for formal ceremonies and weekly chapel services, which are not well-attended. Outlying churches have less than eighty attendees in worship each Sunday. Students use Sundays to sleep or meet friends for brunch. Families from different countries often are not Christians. University Church itself remains hidden two blocks from the main thoroughfare and makes little attempt to be noticed. The location of the church itself reinforces its self-imposed inward focus and its irrelevance to the university and city culture functioning at a fast pace around it.

Influences of the university and the multicultural neighborhoods in the area provide a snapshot of living in postmodern context. Neighborhood cultures change quickly, university students finish courses and move away while new students arrive, teaching and research have a competitive edge that keeps up and attempts to surpass other research centers. Multitasking, high energy, fast-paced social lives and a sense of adventure characterize the populations surrounding the university. Spirituality and support communities meet in homes or public spaces as people find common interests and desire deeper spiritual experiences. Local, long-term residents themselves participate in this cultural milieu, dealing with overcrowded streets and high levels of noise at all hours in exchange for the stimulating, fast-paced lifestyle in the area.

University Church, in the midst of this vibrant university-based culture, quietly carries on with its study and liturgy. If an outsider decides to join the congregation, then members will incorporate him or her into their way of church life. The minister, on the other hand, desires to expand the church's consciousness about theological diversity and interreligious dialogue, leading in time to engagement in the surrounding culture and a ministry that is relevant to the needs of people who live and work only a few hundred feet away.

Congregational Preparation

First, University Church must be willing to think about its own situation in realistic terms by facing "the brutal facts." The congregation is approaching paralysis with a crumbling building on its hands and no means of repair. If Rev. Clare can convince members to name the church's internal culture—its unspoken myths, behaviors, and assumptions about itself—the congregation may begin thinking about fundamental changes required for survival. In time, University Church can move through the wilderness toward transformation. The scenario-building process only works if members are capable of self-assessment and show a desire to embrace new possibilities based on what they do well.

University Church has a history of living in an ethos of biblical inquiry. They also prefer to be an intellectual enclave in the midst of a vibrant neighborhood, implying that they value their own relationships and intellectual endeavors above being church in the world. They may be able to shift this sense of inquiry to a broader understanding of ministry within the area. If Rev. Clare is successful in helping the congregants name their difficult dilemma and face the subconscious behaviors that helped them get there, then she can invite them into the process of looking with hope to the future in light of the great commandment. She also can facilitate discussion about what University Church does well: biblical study and teaching. To do so, Rev. Clare chooses a small group of members and invites an external participant to initiate the scenario-building process. This external voice, a colleague or perhaps the university chaplain, will bring a fresh perspective to the conversation as the group thinks about its focal issue in Step One of the scenario-building process.

Scenario-building

Initially, Step One calls for naming a focal issue. In University Church's case, the scenario-building group is clear about attending to survival rather than creating a new ministry based on a discernment of call for the church. Survival for them translates into finding funding for building repair. Any additional money will target organ repair. However, Rev. Clare keeps the great commandment texts before the small group as well as the entire congregation in hopes that a survival mindset may in time yield to meaningful ministry in the area.

Step Two requires the scenario-building group to pay attention to University Church's surroundings. The group thinks about both its own geographical and social context as well as current events that make an impact on the university community. Members of the entire church gather data through observation and news releases over a period of three to six months and add to the group's collection. The group does not analyze the information, but simply compiles and organizes it. The facilitator keeps momentum alive by asking for congregational input and help to gather the data that will be useful. Rev. Clare refers to relevant news events and reflects theologically on her own observations in sermons and through prayer during worship services.

University Church members discover that research breakthroughs in the medical field, experiments in engineering, and the introduction of new young authors to the literary world all are taking place in their parish. Hospitals in the area receive wounded from war on a regular basis. Muslim, Hindu, and Buddhist worship and meditation spaces advertise their services for students. Tourists visit the university shopping area in growing numbers every year. Human demographics change on a yearly basis. Old buildings themselves change hands as they are converted from churches to restaurants, from pubs to housing. Banks on every other street corner carry multiple currencies at all times. Overcrowding, pollution, and noise levels continue to be issues of concern for the neighborhood. Art and cultural museums connect to the campus and are within walking distance of the church.

This panoply of facts provides a good cross-section for contextual analysis by University Church's scenario-building group. Next, in Step Three, group members think together about the forces or influences that lie behind their list of observations and facts. The university's expansion seems to be a driving force for the area's growth. Student enrollment grows in scientific, medical, and engineering fields each year because the university's reputation as a world leader in these areas attracts students and professors from around the globe. Multicultural neighborhoods and supporting infrastructures for foreigners and immigrants grow accordingly. Multicultural neighborhoods change the local culture to micro-cultures in a university-based context. The increase in student and teacher populations leads to housing shortages and creates needs for more space for university buildings. Property values rise every year. Public transportation and cars clog roads, discharging significant air pollution, and tourists add to crowded conditions. The area is thriving economically based on retail shopping and university investment. At the same time, the area also is being challenged to use resources prudently in a stressful, fast-paced, competitive environment.

Step Four ranks the forces and influences named in Step Three according to their importance for University Church: growth of the university, growth of a variety of micro-cultures including differing customs and languages, increasing presence of many faith traditions, increasing crowding, pollution, noise, and housing shortages. The group pays attention to the most important two or three forces.

In Step Five, the facilitator keeps the top two or three forces before the group and invites them to begin imagining futures in narrative form based on the previous step, as well as on their earlier theological reflection and their understanding of what University Church does best. Three scenarios emerge.

Scenario One: University Church focuses initially on survival by opening its building to university activities. The university contracts to pay a set fee for church use and to conduct meetings, sponsor concerts, perform poetry readings, or run other programs within particular guidelines established by University Church. Activities sponsored by the university would need to be accompanied by university custodial services. Should the university desire to have organ concerts, it would pay for organ repair. University Church retains control of the use of the building with the understanding that the university can use the building at times specified within the guidelines and never during pre-scheduled worship services. University Church becomes visible to the surrounding community, contributes space needed by the university, and covers costs to remain open. In time, University Church becomes a well-known venue for cultural events and promotion of the arts. The church begins to sponsor its own public lectures on the history of the Ancient Near East and origins of scriptural texts.

Scenario Two: University Church puts its building on the market. The university and a contractor both offer to buy University Church, bidding against each other, but naming prices that are below appraisal value. The university would like to convert the church into a concert and lecture hall, closing off the back of the sanctuary to build music practice rooms. The contractor would like to remodel the entire church while keeping its foundation and windows intact and create a trendy restaurant and club, targeting young adults and university students of all ages. Money from the sale to either party would be used to support mission projects sponsored by the denomination. University Church decides to sell the building to the university because the university will uphold a musical tradition of high standard and promote learning and study, prized by church members. Church members agree that they will disperse and attend other local churches based on their personal choices.

Scenario Three: University Church offers to partner with the university to sponsor and house student religious organizations, providing space for gatherings, programs, and study. The university would be welcome to build and run a coffee house in the basement area. University Church invites interfaith dialogue, theological panels on current ethical issues, and conversations about the nature of God and violence in the world. With university funding, University Church creates meditation spaces for different religious traditions and a coffeehouse atmosphere for socializing or studying. Sunday mornings remain open for different Christian groups to lead worship in partnership with a part-time or student minister, hired by University Church. Faculty representatives from the university would relate to each religious group. All groups would be accountable to both the university and University Church in terms of appropriate building use and programming. Current church members could attend worship either when the student minister scheduled services or move to other area congregations.

Scenario Four: Rev. Clare leaves and University Church calls a new minister who focuses on evangelism and charismatic preaching combined with traditional rituals. The church begins to grow. The minister calls on neighborhood groups and invites them to participate in creative worship, incorporating jazz one week and medieval chant the next. The organ is removed and its parts are sold. Some members leave the church and others embrace the minister's views on postmodern styles of leadership. Those who stay find a niche through teaching classes in theology and church history with new participants. Attention to upgrading the building wanes, though repairs occur as needed until attendance becomes large enough to begin remodeling. New attendees invite their friends, including university students and professors; the church continues to grow and eventually thrive, becoming known as a creative, multicultural community embracing diversity.

Step Six places these four scenarios alongside the focal issue established in Step One. University Church names its main focus as survival, with far-reaching hopes of thriving as it did in the late nineteenth and early twentieth centuries. Scenario Two does not match the initial aim, though circumstances in the scenario may occur nonetheless. Scenario One addresses survival but does not change the mindset of church members, who retain as much control over their building as possible, maintaining it for as long as possible. This option shows incremental change. Scenario Three requires a new view of ministry, a conversion of focus from maintenance to adventure as Christians reach out to peoples of different faiths. Living into the post-Christendom, postmodern times requires a change of heart in a congregation, followed by commitment to flexible development of new ministries. This option is transformative. Scenario Four introduces change in leadership resulting in congregational growth. The church remains focused on inviting Christians to attend its services in its building and puts the onus on the new minister to increase participation and giving. This option is incremental with potential to be transforming.

Step Seven invites both the congregation and the scenario-builders to stay attuned to the possibilities that open as the future unfolds.

The group continues to observe data and news items, reflecting on what they see both theologically and practically. They take time for discernment about what God's call might be for them. Rev. Clare introduces evening prayer services for the congregation to experience *temenos* and *kairos* essential for group discernment. As possibilities introduce themselves to the expectant congregation within a few months, members begin to align the signposts with a scenario or parts of different scenarios that the group has created. This alignment continues through their life together as the process of discovery creates an ongoing journey with God. They are becoming Process-Church, ready to co-create the future with God based on thoughtful, reflective responses as God's perpetual call evolves.

City Church

City Church, built in the 1920s with subsequent small additions and a parsonage next door, sits in a transitional neighborhood where large, brick century homes have been divided into apartments. The nearest church is a Pentecostal congregation two blocks away. Several buildings around the church are boarded shut. Within three blocks, new condominium buildings are replacing old houses as re-gentrification of the neighborhood begins. The church itself is a three-story brick building, with an interior built in a semi-circular style. A balcony connected to seven classrooms on the second level surrounds a common room for social gatherings and meetings. The sanctuary seats two hundred, houses an old organ that barely functions and a raised platform for worship leaders. The minister, Rev. David, leads worship with two part-time staff members and volunteer scripture readers, delivering the sermon on the floor level amongst the attendees. Rev. David recruits musicians for worship on a weekly basis.

City Church describes itself as multicultural, with a mission to be in solidarity with the poor and homeless throughout the week. This mission translates into providing clothing and hot meals on Tuesdays, Thursdays, and Sunday mornings. On Sundays after breakfast, anyone from the area who wishes to attend worship is welcome if he or she follows one rule: one may not sleep in the pews during worship.

Worship attendance consists of thirty members, and as many guests from the hot breakfast and clothes closet who decide to stay for the service. The sanctuary may have seventy people in the pews on any given Sunday. Rev. David leads a flexible, interactive worship service, making space for guests who occasionally wish to share impromptu testimonials with the congregation.

City Church's membership declines yearly, though attendance remains steady despite high turnover of attendees. Church members spend time connecting with homeless people of all ages; staff members know many street people and other homeless visitors by name and welcome them to the church. When there is any behavior that threatens the safety of others present, staff members invite perpetrators to leave. The staff does not hesitate to call the police if necessary, though they rarely need to do so. The majority of adults, youth, and families attending meals and requesting clothing are African-American, followed by Caucasian and Latino/Latina persons in smaller numbers.

Suburban churches have been invited to partner with City Church by providing financial support, serving meals, and staffing the clothes room. The staffing calendar is well-organized; suburban church groups serve anywhere from monthly to once or twice each year. Rev. David keeps the name of City Church in front of colleagues staffing churches in suburbia on a regular basis. Suburban ministers and congregations express relief to Rev. David about having a local mission project that requires little organization from their own membership. Further, the denomination applauds the ministry, showcasing City Church when addressing justice ministries. Rev. David assumes that these groups do not understand the meaning of working for justice. He does not attempt to teach congregations or denominational leaders about immersing themselves in situations that are different than theirs as a means of learning to respect strangers whom Christians call neighbors. He remains grateful for the financial support and willing workers and does not have the energy to educate.

City Church knows that it is sharing in a much-needed ministry in its neighborhood. However, Rev. David spends a great deal of his time pursuing financial support from churches and foundations to keep the doors of the church open. He is tired. He has a high turnover of part-time paid staff and cannot afford to increase staff salaries or provide staff benefits. Suburban churches are generous as long as their own budgets can sustain charitable giving; most of this money is used to pay bills and provide for staff. Rev. David knows that he will not be able to continue the ministry much longer without increasing staff workloads and finding new ways to finance the repairs needed to maintain the old building. He himself has opted to earn a minimal salary for the sake of the ministry. His wife provides enough income for their living expenses. Nonetheless, Rev. David feels in need of a sabbatical—at the very least—and intermittently thinks about early retirement. He does not leave for fear that the congregation will close because they cannot afford to keep the building up to code and pay a fair salary to a minister at the same time.

An Ethic of Inquiry for City Church

Theological Reflection

The gospel stories show Jesus teaching the affluent and powerful how to be servants to the poor and marginalized. He tells the rich man to give up what he has and become a follower (Lk. 18:22). To the disciples' consternation, he speaks with a woman considered unclean who draws water from a well during the time of day when she will not be ridiculed by her neighbors (Jn. 4:1–30). He eats with tax collectors, Roman outcasts by Jewish standards (Lk. 5:27–32). Jesus also speaks to the marginalized, inviting them to have faith and be healed, to take up their mats and walk (Mk. 2:1–12). All of these acts of Jesus are witnessed by the general public and heard by those who hold power in the temple.

Prophetic leadership challenges the powerful and the wealthy to think about their roles in the realm of God. After Jesus tells the parable of the Samaritan who provides for an injured foreigner, he addresses the question: Who is my neighbor? Here, Jesus provides the radical notion of love for one's enemies as well as for strangers and friends (Lk. 6:27).

The connection between suburban churches that have financial stability and metro church ministry in economically challenged urban neighborhoods provides a vehicle for learning the lesson Jesus repeatedly taught during his ministry. It is easy to fall into two traps, however. First, ministry opportunities for suburban churches at City Church often are chosen to alleviate the guilt of the more affluent middle and upper classes. Second, when racial-ethnic differences exist, suburban Caucasian churches can claim their own work as proof of overcoming racist attitudes. Rev. David notes that many volunteers have a notion of working out their own redemption through volunteering at City Church. This opportunity to volunteer supplies an easy means of giving time or money. This work for redemption reveals a theological issue regarding the great commandment. What one is called to do with resources and in relationships connects with one's motives for loving "neighbor": stranger, enemy, friend, "other."

Establishing an ethic of inquiry for City Church would be more widely effective if suburban church volunteers were invited into the conversation. In addition to those who work as volunteers based on their own sense of guilt, also some privileged persons have grappled with the meaning of service to neighbor. In addition, others have challenged social and economic systems that create echelons of wealth and poverty in the first place. These servants focus on wholeness and health as goals for people who live in wealth or in poverty; their prayer is that the poor have a chance to reach their potential by gaining voice and means of living with resources necessary for holism. Likewise, the rich have opportunity to adopt new notions of stewardship and equity. Regular conversations with Rev. David, the staff at City Church, and suburban churches' constituencies would provide *temenos* and *kairos* opportunities for challenging personal and systemic racism and classism based on the biblical example of Jesus' relationships.

This theological concern is also a personal spiritual one for Rev. David. How much does Rev. David give of himself without giving himself completely away? What exactly does laying down one's life or losing one's life to find it mean? Is there a point when a boundary is reached before nothing is left in him to give? Might he too need to pursue wholeness? Rev. David struggles with the gospel messages to the rich and to the poor. By neighborhood standards, he is rich. By suburban standards, he is poor. Ultimately, he knows he is called to love the stranger and work with the poor. He also is called to be a whole person himself so that he has the energy and right spirit from which to serve.

The theological concerns surrounding disparity of wealth focus on both local and global levels. It is easy for financially comfortable congregations to become distracted by extreme poverty on a different continent and lose sight of the local poor whom City Church serves. Poverty is relative to one's own economic and social location until poverty reaches the threshold where basic nutrition, health, and shelter needs are not being met. This poverty is absolute. Media regularly flash pictures and sound-bytes of people who live in extreme or absolute poverty, desensitizing middle and upper classes to the struggle whole populations experience on a daily basis. The problem becomes so vast and so minimized at the same time that the affluent can feel helpless in the midst of the need and therefore choose not to serve at churches like City Church at all.

City Church in its current state cannot be a significant influence in changing systems that perpetuate poverty. The church is not taken seriously as a body that has enough clout or expertise to alleviate poverty. Desensitized Christian middle and upper classes have trouble empathizing with people attending City Church, even if some sit on denominational or secular boards and agencies working for the poor because of a vague need to "do something." They often cannot see how their churches can make any more difference than local, national, or global agencies. However, transformation of hearts to be in solidarity with the poor connected with City Church requires not only writing checks, serving soup once a month, and passing resolutions but immersing oneself in the cultures and conversations of people living in poverty in the City Church neighborhood. Jesus walked with the poor and outcast for a time, accused of touching the untouchables and healing them, with the challenge for them to go forth and make a new life in faith. This notion of solidarity with the poor requires a "walking with" as well as attention to opening doors for the poor in ways people in need can control ultimately.

Congregational Preparation

Rev. David knows that the ongoing viability of City Church's ministry with the poor and the homeless is in question despite its positive impact on the neighborhood. He and the staff are overwhelmed with the daily needs of people living on the streets and at the same time are aware that they are leading a small worshiping congregation that expects Christian education classes and pastoral care. City Church is losing momentum in its ministry as finances decline and energy diminishes.

Rev. David decides that the congregation needs to find a way to live into new paths of being in ministry. He invites a small group of leaders in the congregation, a person who has experienced homelessness, and a member of a local social work agency to work with him on scenario-building for the future of City Church. He and the staff hope that if City Church learns to discern God's call into God's future purposes, then it will find the means to co-create this future in a healthy manner.

Rev. David prepares the congregation and volunteers from suburban churches who wish to participate for the work ahead by initiating theological questions he has faced already. Biblical texts proclaiming good news to the poor have always been the basis for ministry at City Church. What texts would allow City Church to embrace its own wholeness and passion for ministry? Does love for neighbor simply mean food and clothing provision? How can ministry complement resources available? Will God provide more resources if City Church pays attention to God's call?

As Rev. David facilitates discussion with members and volunteers, he prepares them for the scenario-building process by asking about ministry passions that surface in the congregation. He also inquires of members what their assumptions about the poor might be, what their behaviors regarding service mean, and how they understand their role in the neighborhood. By inquiring about and naming the internal culture, Rev. David helps people see what myths they hold to be true regarding their connections with neighbors and their understanding of ministry.

Finally, Rev. David describes the process ahead, warning of a wilderness experience through which people must walk if they are to orient themselves to God's unfolding future. This wilderness might bring a chaotic time, but the congregation has known chaos before. To connect people with the process in the midst of impending wilderness, Rev. David invites the congregation and volunteers to give input to the scenario-building group as it conducts its work. He asks members to collect facts, local stories, and information portrayed in the news to add to the group's data. He himself will initiate prayer groups to support the process of City Church's work as the congregation learns to live into God's call as co-creators of the unfolding future.

Scenario-building

The group begins the scenario process by naming the focal issue facing them. Passion and call indicate that the congregation wishes to continue being in ministry with the poor from the current City Church venue while at the same time finding financial support for building repair, staff salaries, and, most importantly, the ministry itself. Members also would like to make a difference in the wider public regarding socioeconomic systems that keep the poor living in poverty.

The scenario-process is initiated by the group collecting information about demographics in the neighborhood and also in the city. They are aware that many homeless people are not accounted for in studies about the homeless; most census work occurs one day a year during winter, so an accurate picture of homelessness data does not exist. However, income level information, employment rates, and social service networks available give indications of the concerns facing the city. The entire congregation pays attention to the local and national news, noting where governments are focusing their social emphases. They also pay attention to grassroots movements started by peace and justice groups and social networks. Scenario-builders themselves note the cost of living in their area, the average wage, and the numbers of people who have mental and physical challenges and/or illnesses who cannot afford housing or institutional care. Everyone listens to the stories about homeless shelters and violence against homeless people on the streets. Participants pay attention to the homeless cultures and sleeping areas, discovering that women and men have different fears about living on the streets or about taking advantage of sheltered housing. They discover too that more youth and families are homeless than first perceived. The congregation and volunteers hear about loss of dignity, invisibility, ongoing illness, rape, prostitution, violence from police officers, disappearances, and death. They also hear testimonies, gossip, and moments of joy.

The group categorizes the information it has gathered in conjunction with the congregation from three to six months of observation. Then it meets to think about the forces that lie behind the data. For instance, government programs geared toward the poor often are driven by public opinion and therefore are unlikely to exhibit longevity. Distrust of the local government's and churches' abilities to address the needs of the poor has led to a local resurgence of grassroots organizing and social justice activity in the city. The declining infrastructure for the poor and homeless based on withdrawal of governmental involvement leaves not-for-profit and private organizations with the responsibility of establishing shelters and building low-income housing. Churches slowly are being invited to participate with agencies to do this work. Violence against homeless people stems from territorial claims by other street groups or individuals; it also can be a way officials take out their anger and frustration or express their power without repercussion.

City Church members conclude that the greatest force behind the facts they have collected is the denial by the majority of the population in the city that there is a homelessness or at-risk problem that affects thousands of people. They speculate that lower income people feel too close to poverty and therefore do not want to address it in any systemic way. Middle and upper income people either feel guilt, which leads to denial, or simply cannot see the problem because they are never exposed to it themselves. Self-justification based in class privilege often portrays itself through general accusations such as identifying all poor people as lazy, not interested in education or self-advancement, but instead living off the tax dollars of the rich and middle class.

City Church scenario-builders also have been clear for a long time that the poor are less likely to be Caucasian than African-American or recent immigrants from Latino, Caribbean, or African countries. Race privilege for whites keeps power in white hands; offering opportunity to equalize power would require significant transformation of those who hold power currently.

Finally, the group noted in their own experience and by reading gathered data that more men than women live on the streets. They concluded from the stories they heard that women find ways to shelter with other women, friends, or relatives so that they do not experience the dangers of theft, rape, or murder. Women with children work even harder to find shelter, often living in cars or hotel rooms if they can find someone to pay. Therefore, homeless rates for women and children are very difficult to track, but they suspect that single mothers are the dominant group experiencing poverty. At this point, the scenario-builders share their findings with the congregation, focusing the prayer services around these issues.

Once the data has been gathered and interpreted, the City Church group ranks the forces behind their information in order of importance. First, they name power inequities and lack of access for poor people to health care and good education as the primary force that perpetuates poverty. The second force behind the data is a pervasive public opinion that denies that poverty has a racial-ethnic aspect to it. The group also focuses on guilt issues experienced by the affluent as a contributor to this denial.

Creation of scenarios follows as the group bears in mind the great commandment, the lack of influence City Church has in challenging poverty, data collected, and the driving forces that lie behind the information. This step develops the narratives for scenarios, with focus on brainstorming and creating imaginative possibilities.

Scenario One: Rev. David and the staff decide that they are too exhausted to continue leading the local ministry, the money runs out, and the church closes. The homeless and the poor are on their own to find a way to survive. City Church members attempt to find another church that has a similar ministry in the neighborhood and invite them to put their efforts into maintaining relationships with City Church's constituency. They contact the suburban churches that were helping City Church and repeat the invitations to help with the ministry in a new location. Several suburban churches accept the invitation and continue volunteering in the new location. Many persons who remain homeless or in need find a way to the new location and the ministry continues without Rev. David and the original staff present there.

Scenario Two: Upon hearing that City Church might close, a donor who has been invited by Rev. David to support the ministry in the past comes forward with an endowment proposal, supplying enough money to continue the ministry. The donor offers the support contingent upon City Church working with City Hall to develop additional health and welfare programs for persons who have mental health challenges and for persons who work but do not make a living wage. The donor also would like to support City Church in developing public education forums about the systemic nature of poverty. City Church accepts the proposal and contacts local grassroots groups for aid in finding a strategic contact at City Hall. Rev. David refocuses his time from serving meals to creating a network in the neighborhood and building influence with City Hall administrators and local politicians. The support money allows the church program to continue and the staff to be paid fair salaries.

Scenario Three: City Church decides to close, but not before they have established networks with other churches and agencies to provide basic needs. City Church members create a homeless "reverse ministry," where the homeless and the poor themselves lead street worship, forming a different kind of community in the neighborhood. When the weather precludes street worship, the homeless gather in area churches for services during the week. Local churches and agencies are invited to participate. Rev. David serves on staff of another urban church and coordinates the reverse ministry with participants who show leadership and consistency in attendance. Suburban churches are invited to come and be part of the congregation and to fellowship with worship leaders after the service. Donations will be welcome to continue the reverse ministry. In time, when there are enough resources and financial support, area churches can approach civic leaders with seed money for an affordable, safe housing initiative.

Each of these scenarios names possibilities for the future. The first does not connect with the focal issue, though it solves the ministry issue with which City Church grapples. Abandoning the ministry and reorganizing it from another venue does not revitalize the work so much as simply moves it.

The latter two scenario narratives require a shift in focus by Rev. David, the staff, and members of City Church. These two narratives connect with the initial focus issue regarding enhancement of the ministry with the poor. The second scenario in particular adds the final component, directly addressing the call to build influence with the public so that discussions about systemic poverty become educational public forums. This scenario narrative has potential to be transformative for the church, neighborhood, suburban volunteers, and the city itself. The scenario-building group has the choice to re-work the first narrative so that it aligns more closely with the initial focal issue.

To live into any of these scenarios will require attention to unfolding events that suggest what God's purposes for the future are. Signals from the neighborhood or from donor churches or individuals will provide hints for the congregation as it actively watches and listens on its path through the wilderness to a new place. In time, the interconnection of City Church's attention to its context and the constant creative work of God in the world points toward elements of one or more scenarios. Scenarios are modified as needed and work begins within a few months as the path becomes clearer.

Rev. David and the staff continue to involve the congregation in prayer groups, emphasizing that the great commandment can be lived wherever people go. They also invite members to try worship events on the streets. Conversations about public initiatives continue in the church as members watch signposts. As the future unfolds, they continue to think through new scenarios prayerfully while reflecting on God's actions. Whatever comes, the members will respond faithfully because they have already named possibilities. Their willingness to live into the process of co-creation by reinventing themselves opens City Church to a new way of claiming new life. They are becoming Process-Church.

Field Church

Field Church, a white clapboard one-room building with a small kitchen and fellowship area in the basement, stands firmly in the midst of farm fields at the crossroads of two county roads. The building displays a cornerstone that reads "1901." A gravel parking lot accommodating twenty cars surrounds the church on three sides. One old oak tree stands at the edge of the parking lot; it is the only tree in sight. The nearest neighboring churches exist in town, fifteen miles away.

Field Church employs a bi-vocational minister who spends the majority of his time working as a nurse at a county hospital twenty miles away. Pastor Jon preaches on Sunday mornings to a group of twenty-seven people, depending on the season of the year and the weather conditions. Four farm families of German or Austrian descent and their children attend Field Church. When planting, harvesting, and plowing seasons are at their peak, five to eight people are available on Sunday morning for services and Sunday school immediately following worship. At harvest time, Pastor Jon cancels services and visits families on the farms for lunch or supper instead. There he learns what pastoral concerns have arisen during the week or listens to the local gossip. Pastor Jon has been known to accompany farmers and field hands into the fields to help them with their work.

Field Church members celebrate their history through storytelling and memorial events. They have photographs on the walls of every pastor who has served the church. They display their charter and the one local mission project per year that they support on a bulletin board inside the front door. The sanctuary has an out-of-tune piano at the front, an altar, and a chair for the pastor. The pastor has been expected to preach without lectern and without notes, from the heart, since the church opened its doors. Emphasis on oral tradition implies that any preacher who needs notes from which to expound on the biblical text does not exhibit signs of the Holy Spirit. Hymns are listed on a board on the wall by the piano and are taken from an early–twentieth-century hymnbook. One or two members of the congregation lead the singing, but few sing loudly. Giving rates and attendance numbers are also posted, comparing the two prior weeks' statistics to each other. The most important aspects of worship for Field Church consist of the announcements and the prayer concerns, each defining the schedule for the upcoming week in terms of activities and community care. Members of Field Church understand the church to be an extension of their weekly farming rhythms, where family gatherings take place on Sundays. Sunday mornings are not considered separate worship events set aside in their lives so much as one aspect of farming life.

Field Church exhibits some anxiety about its future in a declining community. Members think about their lives in economic terms constantly as they watch family farms around them being bought rapidly by large agribusinesses or housing developers. Parents also watch their children leave school and also leave the family farming tradition behind for jobs in suburbia or in urban centers. Members wonder if Pastor Jon can do anything to invite other families into the church so that there is enough money and participation to keep the doors open. They suggest homecoming events, revival services, and special meals that would attract people from the nearest town. Pastor Jon is willing to contribute to these attempts, but does not have the time to plan them. He expresses to a few trusted friends and colleagues that he does not see much hope for this family chapel but will remain present, fulfilling his contract for seven hours per week until the pastoral ministry at Field Church is no longer viable as it stands.

The unique ministry of Field Church is its family chapel focus. Field Church provides a space where farmers feel connected to previous generations and also to a God who provides for them through the land. The worship time is one of the few chances during the week, unless it is winter, to catch up with neighbors and discuss the current weather and soil conditions, set up times to share farm equipment or plan social gatherings and meals together. Field Church is both social connection and symbol of family tradition for the families who attend there.

An Ethic of Inquiry for Field Church

Theological Reflection

The unspoken mission of Field Church is to provide space for people to connect their work with the land and to connect with each other in restful, holy gatherings as part of the week's rhythm. Keeping tradition alive manifests itself in the photographs and important papers in the entryway of the church. Stories about farming in the days of prosperity, when God provided bounty, mix with worries about present sporadic weather patterns. Occasionally, a member will ask Pastor Jon where God's presence might be found for the farmer these days. Pastor Jon tells people to keep praying.

The perceived absence of God when the fields flood or harden in the sun raises issues about the nature of a loving God who abandons the people of the land. Field Church comprehends wilderness living well. Often, they seek loans to subsidize their farms, hoping for a good yield each year. They monitor prices of grain and livestock as the economy shifts or storms destroy crops. Bountiful years bring brief celebration as loans are paid and money can be set aside for the next lean year. God's presence seems to wax and wane in the midst of this wilderness.

The threat of failure stays alive in this wilderness existence. Temptation to sell the family farm stems from a desire to stop worrying each year and to be comfortable in old age. Yet loyalty to the generations of farmers who have lived and breathed with the land keeps families going one year at a time. The people of Field

Church remain close to the cycles of seasons and the natural world, connecting them to indigenous peoples and to their own ancestors, and keeping the reality of earth's provision and harsh scarcity alive. Psalm 8 reassures them that God cares for them and for creation. Matthew 10:26–31 reinforces their own sense of value in the eyes of God, who cares for the sparrow as well as the human being. These texts are printed from time to time in their orders of service as reminders of Field Church families' valuable work in the world.

Yet, questions about why hard-working, faithful people suffer have no resolution at Field Church. Pastor Jon knows better than to give glib responses. He does point out that the people's care for the land, the creation, connects them to God in a unique way. The majority of the population in North America does not understand that land is sacred and to be honored. Almost everyone visits local grocery stores, where food is packaged and easily transported home. Few pay attention to the sources of their food unless they plant small gardens themselves or work with a cooperative farm group. Instead, the desire for agribusiness to harvest crops at low cost and the industry's desire for efficiency and super-foods has led to mass production. Further, genetic alteration of naturally occurring plants and animals removes consumers one step further from the land and its natural gifts. Pastor Jon calls this phenomenon "playing God."

Field Church members are loyal to their farms and to the accompanying traditions. They love God like they love their families; joy, anger, humility, and pride all are expressions of their connection with God. A sense of abandonment in the wilderness balances with the knowledge that the farm is home. Fear of judgment in harsh years balances with experiences of grace in abundant years. Suffering is countered by endurance as families reinforce determination to survive and thrive.

The globalizing world presents another kind of challenge for Field Church. The politics of food distribution affects farmers through government-imposed food-aid programs, farm subsidies that can be inconsistent, and the gourmet food industries established in large cities requiring the best of what is produced hundreds and even thousands of miles away. Cost of transporting food rises when oil prices rise, ultimately causing food prices to rise. When the consumer buys less of the expensive food, farmers cannot make a profit or break even.

As crops become sources of energy and fuel, agribusiness itself will perpetuate the dangers of growing one crop. Pesticides do not prevent insect devastation more than one or two years, so mono-crops invite widespread crop failure. Ultimately, production of food has become market-economy dependent and environmentally unsound. Pollutants affect watersheds and over-farming hastens erosion of land. Yet small family farms believe that they must adopt agribusiness farm practices and products to compete in the business of food production.

Field Church does not wish to involve itself in the politics of food production. Occasionally the farm families respond to the government's or national organizations' appeals to send food to the hungry overseas. They do so, but at a labor and financial cost that organizations do not realize. The Field Church families resent at times that these requests surface without knowledge of the ripple effect such endeavors cause for family farmers.

Field Church members have been listening to other requests as well. Movements addressing immigrant guest worker rights have come to their attention. Issues of living conditions and fair wages for migrant workers have no easy solutions for Field Church farmers who rely on cheap labor so that the farms remain solvent. To make an impact that matters for workers and farmers, Field Church understands that conversations with laborers and justice groups bring informed perspectives on living wages and housing. Because Field Church's members do not have much impact on government leaders, networking with other justice groups is crucial for change.

Pastor Jon is aware that Field Church members are not interested in challenging politics, so he knows that he has a spiritual leadership role to play when addressing worker rights with farmers. He bases his thinking on the great commandment: How does one care for neighbor who is transient and a paid worker? Do migrant workers need to be thought of in a different light? Pastor Jon realizes that these questions are not the only ones facing Field Church.

The influences of the globalized, postmodern world affect farmers' children as they do all other children who have access to television, film, music, and Internet at school or home. The sense of adventure that young adults exhibit reinforces itself through Internet conversations with people their own age who are experiencing very different lives. Increasingly, young adults move away from home, work so that they can travel for a year, and then choose to settle in an urban or suburban area of choice. Some return home, but few return to the Field Church area farms. Family farming traditions passed on to the rising generation are rare.

Congregational Preparation

Pastor Jon is torn about putting time into helping Field Church re-imagine its future. However, his care for the people leads him to see if he can challenge the mindset that calls for endurance to preserve tradition against all odds. To prepare the congregation for the hard work of change, he gathers the farm families together on Sunday after church service for a conversation about God's role in the lives of farmers. Pastor Jon is not setting out to grow the church numerically, but instead to shift its focus so that it becomes a vital movement in the life of the farming community. He refers to the rhythms of the seasons, the different types of work required for each season and also the rhythm of the liturgical year and its corresponding spiritual work. He also introduces the great commandment as part of the biblical injunction to love God, neighbor, and creation in ways that are life-giving for migrant workers and for the land itself.

Pastor Jon invites the congregation to think more deeply with him during worship services and in the fields about God's connection with the people and the land. He pledges to focus sermons and prayers on this connection. Then he requests that the congregation gather for discussions about its future based on the scenario-building process, including a young adult intern majoring in agricultural sciences at a university extension site.

Pastor Jon facilitates their work due to their isolated location and limited resources. He begins by asking the congregation to articulate the facts of farm living, including joys and challenges. Field Church already faces the facts of their future every day, so people can list them easily. They conclude that their church is completely dependent on the farm families remaining on their land. Should the farmers sell to agribusiness or housing developers, the church simply will cease to exist.

Scenario-building

The scenario-building process begins by stating Field Church's focal issue. Members want to keep their farm community, including Field Church, alive. Field Church families express concerns not only about their church closing due to farm sales or as the next generation moves away, they also show sorrow that generations of tradition passed on from their parents and grandparents will not be carried on by their children. Even if the church closes, members wish to keep the family farming ethos alive. They hope to leave a farming legacy as a tribute to long-held family traditions. The future looks bleak. They wish to find new ways to have local investment in their livelihoods. Yet, they love their farms and their families, past and present. That love continues to hold them to the land for as long as they can survive.

Field Church families conduct their own research on a regular basis regarding food prices, production and fuel costs, wages for hired workers, market values of their crops and livestock, as well as the challenge of competing agribusiness that produce the same crops more cheaply. Because a data-gathering mindset already exists, further information about market trends, unexpected events affecting food production, and small farm viability predictions are easy to collect. New information that can have an impact on farmers in the area includes discovering grassroots movements and church attention being given to the issues family farmers face. What groups are paying attention to the same issues that farmers are concerned about? How do agribusiness and government entities respond to these groups? Members of Field Church gather their information and organize it, with special attention given to the news affecting independent farms.

After three to six months, Field Church families and the university intern begin to think together about what forces are affecting the information they have gathered from the news or from grassroots groups' Web sites. They gather at the church for their meetings, because Field Church has always been the community decision-making space.

They discuss how supply and demand for crops affect the market economy; this cause-effect economic structure is the greatest driving force behind farm success or failure in any given year for them. Field Church members believe also that the desire for efficiency at low cost has led to agribusiness and food-altering genetics; pressure to compete to survive, a driving force for family farms, causes Field Church members to adopt these practices and purchase altered seed products despite their discomfort with them.

Members also talk about how people no longer value family businesses and are disconnected from the sources of their food and therefore do not see the issues that farmers face. Field Church meetings consist of conversation about the rhythms of food production and the demand from grocery stores and food suppliers for year-round provisions of seasonal foods thereby relying on foreign markets. They claim that God created seasons for a reason, but human disconnection with these rhythms renders the public unconcerned for the family farm and its ability to produce a variety of seasonal crops in a healthy environment.

Field Church members rank the importance of these two driving forces in the next stage of the process. First, they connect Field Church with the viability of farming. Field Church is space for the "town hall" meeting, providing a sense of God's presence in the midst of their livelihoods. Farmers move to concrete issues, claiming supply and demand as the force of greatest importance. Second, the invisibility of the small, family farm makes it easy for independent farmers to be bought out. Third, the disconnection from the land as a source of life renders food simply a consumer good.

With the ranking of forces behind the data and news collected, Field Church members create scenarios from which to imagine possibilities for their future. They do not divide their church from their farming lives neatly; instead, the natural integration of church as a rhythm of weekly life plays out in the scenario narratives.

Scenario One: Field Church farmers sell their farms to agribusiness or housing developers. Farmers either work for the agribusiness company, leave the area altogether, or, in the case of housing development, choose plots for their own new homes. Field Church remains open if local farmers remain in the area working for an agribusiness company. Otherwise, if the land is sold to developers, the church is abandoned.

Scenario Two: Field Church family farmers refocus their food production into niche farming and developed a cottage industry around specialty foods and cooking, much like many Mennonite and Amish communities. The church's role would be to sponsor festivals that draw people from local towns and more distant cities. Church liturgies and events introduce the public to the blessing of the land, not only in the Field Church area, but through customs learned from throughout the world. An education center housed initially in the Field Church basement, and depending on interest and income, in its own adjacent building, would provide children with hands-on programs about farming and food production. University interns who study the environment, political science, and economics could serve as leaders in the education center's programming, creating gardens that teach about plants and land-use. They also would design age-appropriate opportunities for public participation in farming operations on two acres of land closest to the church. Income from program tuition, festivals, and specialty food sales to the attending public would supplement farmers' income. The great commandment plays out through love of God's creation, drawing people together in a culture of appreciation for the land and for God's bounty. Further, raised public consciousness about environmental issues, stewardship, and blessings of creation results in widespread concern and advocacy for the independent farmer.

Scenario Three: Ministries are introduced for migrant guest workers as they spend the season on local farms. These ministries provide worship opportunities and also training for the workers. Farmers provide small plots of land to workers for permanent housing and personal gardens in exchange for reasonable work for free rent and an additional fair wage. Ministries include culturally appropriate support and liturgy. Funding is provided through a ministry appeal in Field Church's denomination; Pastor Jon makes the case for worker justice and consciousness-raising about sustainable farming to the appropriate leadership in the denomination and to grassroots organizations. To begin the program, donors and grants will be secured through Pastor Jon's efforts. As demand for specialty farming rises, labor-intensive work rises followed by an increase in income, decreasing reliance on grants over time. Guest workers would be welcome to stay as long as feasible.

Each scenario narrative is examined in light of the focal issue named initially. Scenarios that address viability of family farms and preservation of tradition meet the focal issue most closely. All narratives have possibility; but the first does not satisfy the community's desire to keep the farming tradition and Field Church alive. The second requires high energy and investment, changing mindsets and transforming lives, with Field Church as an important component of the scenario.

The third requires high energy and provides a labor solution with long-term gains after short-term struggle. This narrative places Field Church and its pastor at the center of influence for its economic well-being. Only two narratives address the focal issue with positive futures for Field Church, promoting wholeness for the community.

Finally, members of Field Church begin to watch for God's call in the signposts that reveal the future as it becomes the present. This active waiting calls the people into intentional relationship with God as they co-create their future. Their work with scenario-building helps them recognize the signs of possibilities before them, thereby intensifying awareness and hope. Pastor Jon and several church leaders initiate conversations with the nearest university and with the town, introducing two of the three scenario ideas to each, modifying the narratives as appropriate. Pastor Jon also focuses his worship services on the liturgical year, weaving liturgical and environmental rhythms together in new rituals and emphases on the blessings of God. He reinforces the understanding of God's love meeting people where they are, inviting response so that God and the people of Field Church become Process-Church, co-creating an imaginative future based on wholeness and love.

Suburban Church

Denominationally affiliated Suburban Church is situated in an upper-middle class area five miles outside an urban center's city limits. New housing developments spring up yearly in the area, ranging from condominiums around golf communities to large estates selling for several millions of dollars. Medical, computer, and communications technologies contribute to growth in the urban center, drawing large corporate headquarters to be established near the urban center's highway outer belt. Road construction cannot keep up with traffic levels, resulting in daily traffic gridlock during morning and evening commutes. Public transportation remains limited to the immediate edges of the city.

Suburban infrastructure lags behind housing development. Large new schools, medical facilities, water, electricity lines, and shopping centers follow the developing housing areas, but high demand cannot be met until these infrastructures are built. Farmers are selling parcels of land yearly for high returns. Wildlife is being pushed out of the area and viable water supplies are strained. In the midst of the development, large new churches, mostly independent rather than denominationally based, establish themselves in the midst of residential areas and close to well-traveled highways.

Suburban Church itself was built twenty years ago, at the beginning of the population influx. At that time, the church parking lot was flanked on two sides by middle-class homes on half-acre lots. The remaining adjacent land was wooded. Four years ago, the woods were removed and new houses constructed, sitting on two to five-acre lots. These homes sold for $350,000–$500,000. Suburban Church finds itself land-locked. Its members wonder why they did not attempt to buy the wooded land when it was for sale.

Suburban Church records an average Sunday attendance of 540, with mostly Caucasian families present. In the past twenty years, members have seen an ebb-and-flow in attendance, which they attribute to the pastoral style of the senior minister. They also are aware of the transient nature of the congregation's participants. Founding members have retired and have a "hold the fort" mentality as young families move in and out of the area. Three full-time staff include the Senior Minister, Office Administrator, and Christian Education and Youth Ministries Director. Three part-time staff care for pre-school and after-school programs, and three additional part-time staff manage financial and membership records, home visitations, and custodial services. Full-time staff meets weekly and the entire staff meets monthly to update each other on parish concerns and events.

Suburban Church prides itself on its 160 programs, mostly created and staffed by volunteers. Monthly congregational giving keeps these ministries afloat, falling short only during the summer months when as much as half the congregation leaves for vacation. Educational and social events programs constitute the main emphasis of the ministries in the church. Evangelism and social justice ministries are delegated to working groups, which invite the congregation to participate in each group's endeavors four-to-six times per year. Suburban Church is busy throughout the week with its pre-school and after-school programs; many children there do not attend the church but will take part in summer vacation Bible school when offered in an intensive format.

Rev. Suzanne, the Senior Minister, knows that Suburban Church seems to be "holding its own" as its statistics are analyzed by the denomination. The congregation has shown no particular growth in attendance for ten years despite the growing neighborhood, but it has shown no significant decline either. The frequency of young families moving into the area and then leaving it again within one or two years continues to rise. This high turnover of the housing market results in ongoing searches by staff for new volunteers to support church programming. In addition, finding volunteers who remain consistent for a year is becoming increasingly difficult. Long-term members express their tiredness. New participants live with schedules that require fitting church life in with family life: jobs, sports, school, social events, extended family vacation, work, and maintaining a household. Many mothers and an occasional father in the community work full-time in the home, raising children, volunteering in civic organizations of choice, and supporting local school and sporting events.

Rev. Suzanne also watches the new church starts in the area. She notes that their evangelism programs are well-organized and strongly supported by the congregations. These new churches invite charismatic pastors to be their leaders. They also employ staff from within their own membership rather than conducting job searches when vacancies occur. She wonders if these churches have an advantage in the area, because they do not make mistakes when hiring staff for particular positions; they already know the capabilities of those they hire and, therefore can perpetuate the ministries they want without much need for staff training. Rev. Suzanne also admits some envy for these independent churches. They do not have to answer to a denomination and can be highly flexible in their educational and evangelism approaches. She believes that they do not have to be accountable for attendance and effectiveness to anyone but themselves and, therefore, do not feel the same kind of professional pressure to succeed as she does while living within her denominational guidelines and evaluative structures.

Rev. Suzanne and Rev. Ben, the Christian Education and Youth Ministries Director, have frequent conversations about the nature of ministry in Suburban Church. With high turnover of volunteers, unreliable attendance at events, and an exhausted older membership, the model of programming currently in place at Suburban Church seems to be broken. The staff feels overwhelmed with the workload and the volunteers have an increasingly high drop out rate. The energy of the congregation wanes as Suburban Church tries to address perceived neighborhood desires for programming at the church that fits busy lifestyles. Further, church conflicts are increasing within committees and among volunteers. The stress level of parishioners attending Suburban Church has been rising steadily since Rev. Suzanne arrived three years ago. She and Rev. Ben share the opinion that Suburban Church's ministry is suffering, but they cannot quite pinpoint the reasons for their trepidation. They suspect that the level of involvement by families in the area does not leave much time for attention to ministry. The attendance and giving numbers look steady; the spirit of the congregation, including volunteers and paid staff, seems frenzied and tired.

Ethic of Inquiry for Suburban Church

Theological Reflection

Suburban Church maintains itself as a viable organization despite high turnover of participants. Maintenance of church programs and attendance indicates institutional solvency but also suggests spiritual decline in the faith community. Numerous programs that are difficult to staff and the "tired" feeling within the church imply that congregants do not find energizing meaning in the ministries offered. Increasing conflict speaks of members' fatigue and sense of adding "one more thing" to busy schedules. Pastors Suzanne and Ben wonder how the work of the church differs from secular activities in parishioners' minds.

Suburban Church, like all Christian communities, has a call to share the good news of God's love as an extension of the incarnation of God in Christ. The nature of the good news in growing suburbia where people are busy and stressed is to help people let go of activities that do not provide meaning to their lives and the lives of others. Rev. Suzanne hopes to introduce a way to quiet the frenzy and focus the spirit so that people's deepest yearnings can be named, perhaps for the first time. Opening space, *temenos,* for the inner being to connect with God takes intentional time, *kairos,* for sitting in the presence of the Holy. From this inner being stems the actions of ministry.

In communities where success is measured by income, appearance, and prestige, this inner being remains elusive if not invisible for many. Given the chance, God connects with the inner being, exposing the scarcity of meaning in frenzied programs. Finding the "mighty silence" or the "still small voice" (1 Kings 19:11–15) brings forth new understanding of life's purposes in the midst of the whirlwind of activity.

Suburban Church equates abundance with prosperity and activity. Prosperity as a definition of success does not stem only from secular standards, however. A popular message in many Christian circles portrays God blessing those who are favored for their piety or their works with prosperous returns. The parable of the talents is one biblical story cited for such theological claims (Mt. 25:14–30).

In a capitalist society, this notion of prosperity translates to expectation of reward for the competitive best. This society perpetuates the myth of entitlement held by a particular race, gender, and economic class, where prosperity remains a "given" for some and scarcity a "given" for others, often perceived to be so at God's sanction.

Yet true abundance, spiritual abundance, looks different than entitlement, material accumulation, and church attendance numbers. Abundance means people living simpler, quieter lives. Responding to inner callings focuses on ministries that make a difference in the world around them rather than supplementing their own lives with church programs. Success redefined from prosperity to abundance of radical love for God, self, and neighbor turns the focus of Suburban Church from the pressure of secular or denominational success to faithfulness to the call of God.

The Revs. Suzanne and Ben face change themselves. The pressure to produce church statistics and report them to their denomination on a yearly basis as indications of growth or decline keeps them focused on attendance, programs, and giving rates. While important, this emphasis on statistics leaves little room for creating space and time for theological and spiritual reflection. As leaders, they find it difficult to be prophetic, let alone creative, in the midst of organizational anxiety and fatigue. The question for church professionals is how to stand in the midst of denominationally defined success based on secular criteria and yet maintain faithful leadership based on context and call.

Congregational Preparation

Initiating Suburban Church's scenario work is the most difficult of all the church settings named thus far because the church experiences a level of comfort that allows it to live in denial longer than the other churches facing closure. A sense of urgency does not exist; it is the perception of the ministers that the church is heading for difficulty that spurs the scenario-building exercises rather than a widespread concern about the church's future. In addition, loyalty to Suburban Church remains low for most because of their transient lives. Nonetheless, willingness of members to trust their leaders allows the scenario-building endeavor to take place and be incorporated into the church.

Both clergy know that the institutional nature of Suburban Church needs to change so that ministry provides meaningful connection to people's needs rather than their desires. They decide to invite the congregation to think about its internal culture and the assumptions about ministry residing there. The congregation understands that they are not being asked to create a new program so much as to discover a new outlook on how to be faithful community in a different way. To enter this reflective time, the congregation agrees to alter its focus for an initial preparatory year that leads eventually to the scenario-building exercise. Many congregants are willing to suspend involvement in a variety of current ministries to participate in small groups for this purpose.

Rev. Suzanne works with Rev. Ben to identify a small group of leaders within Suburban Church who have shown initiative and disciplined follow-through in the past. They meet with this group to discuss what kinds of preparation will be needed for the congregation as a whole as Suburban Church moves into a process that rethinks how it understands ministry. The clergy agree to focus sermons on the great commandment's challenge and blessing for churches like Suburban Church, inviting people into a time of reflection about how they see God's love working in the world. They refocus small groups from programmatic or study emphases to spiritual practices based on Jesus' commandment. Sunday school classes for all ages will devise their curricula around the great commandment at the same time. Rev. Ben is willing to aid leaders in finding resources and thinking through the year through several workshops and one short retreat.

Rev. Suzanne decides that she will not only focus her preaching on stories that illustrate the great commandment close to home and all over the world, she will extend invitations to guest preachers who have their own stories to tell from immersions in other countries as well as their experiences in the local community. Rev. Suzanne also hopes to introduce catered church-wide dinner events that underline the highly connected, globalized world through featuring foods and customs foreign to Suburban Church. She knows that there are parishioners who would be interested in providing input from their own ancestral heritages as well. Dinners would be followed by contemplative worship and times for discernment about ministry in today's secular, globalized, highly technological society. Emphasis on God's love and desire for human beings to love each other, luring congregants into a different kind of future, remains central to all worship and study.

One to two months after the congregation has moved into its preparatory year structure, Rev. Suzanne asks a colleague from another church to join the scenario-building small group. She also invites another colleague who is an officer in a different denomination to facilitate the process. Rev. Suzanne's goal is to have the congregation doing the work of spiritual discernment alongside the small group so that ongoing input to the scenario-building process can be sustained.

Scenario-building

Scenario-builders know that Suburban Church's understanding of ministry as a plethora of programs is leading to burn out in the congregation. This current practice of ministry also ignores the potential for Suburban Church to answer a particular call from God. Suburban Church has assumed since its inception that relevant programs will bring new members to worship, defining success as numerical increase. The small group sees now that this assumption is not necessarily faithful to God's purposes rather than denominational purposes. They name the focal issue for Suburban Church to be a redefinition of ministry altogether, based on the great commandment.

The denominational facilitator invites members of the group to begin data gathering for the scenario-building endeavor. The group gathers data about Suburban Church and its surrounding environment by surveying the congregation, asking pre-set questions that they have devised themselves. Scenario-builders in this case are curious about what drains the community and what provides energy. They record responses over a period of three months.

The group invites teen leaders to discover what kinds of faith questions and interests their peers at school talk about on a regular basis. The scenario-builders also ask work colleagues and friends who do not attend the church what kinds of pressures daily life presents to families and singles who lived in the area. They ask everyone the question, "What issue or concern keeps you up at night?"

The group notes that working parents do not have enough time with their children, stay-at-home working parents feel like their lives are run by children's schedules almost exclusively, and both groups feel like they live on a boring, high-speed treadmill but are afraid to step off. Surveys from within in the church reveal that attendees do not feel intellectually stimulated nor inspired about the meaning of life. Finally, the research group learns that adults want permission to rest while making sure that their children are being taught to live ethical lives through the local church.

In addition to qualitative surveys, for three more months the group also researches demographics regarding housing expansion and populations moving into the area. They combine their data with the input contributed by the congregation from gatherings for discernment about the meaning of the great commandment.

The group collates its data collected over a six-month period and begins to categorize it, analyzing driving forces behind what they gleaned. For example, Suburban Church symbolizes a potential haven for anxious, overworked families. The church is understood not as a countercultural organization that invites participants to work for radical change in the world but as a place to regain strength to face the world. The drive to succeed in the secular world saps the strength of the majority of persons living in the suburban area.

At the same time, the local neighbors do not distinguish Suburban Church's ministry from any other extracurricular activity. The consumer consciousness drives the notion that when one is stressed or questioning, one can find solace or answers at the local church until the next stressful event or question arises. The group finds that in most cases, regular attendance for families occurs because church participation is part of the suburban milieu with the added bonus of providing education about morality for children and youth. Single young adults rarely are seen at church; if they do attend, they do so because they have friends also attending.

Demographics show that as employment opportunities increase in the urban center and an increasing number of companies build headquarters in the area, upper management and executive jobs provide income for higher end housing and a country club social network. The church itself sees evidence of this trend based on the homes built recently on the edge of its parking lot. These new families tend not to attend established churches. If they have young children and choose to attend anywhere, they often find independent churches with facilities for sports and worship with sophisticated technologies that support a high-energy worship service.[5]

Suburban Church scenario-builders conclude that the primary driving force behind the facts is the individual's desire for success in the secular world countered with a need for rest and renewal. Success constitutes raising one's financial status, which directly affects social status. The group further speculates that upper income people have become used to designating what they want in return for their financial support. The consumer mindset hits suburban churches especially hard because of the level of disposable income families accrue; all products desired can be bought, including weddings, funerals, children's and youth programs, as well as pastoral services. A sense of entitlement for ministry services occurs when church attendees contribute anything in the offering plate or volunteer in the church. Volunteer time either constitutes a way of "paying one's dues" rather than giving an offering, "paying back" for blessings or ministerial services, or a sense of "doing the right thing." Volunteers who do not believe that the staff or the congregation appreciate them either leave or complain about the church. Clergy are expected in many cases to be personal family chaplains.

Analysis of the data, mostly narrative in nature, causes the research group to work on self-assessment as well. Rev. Suzanne and the facilitator keep the group focused on the task of scenario-building because it is easy for participants in Suburban Church to name the challenges of the church and become tempted to leave themselves. Rev. Suzanne finds that she must continually rekindle participant interest in a long-term process. She decides to share group findings with the congregation after the scenarios are created, to keep hope alive.

The next step for the group is to rank the forces behind the data in order of importance. The group names first the secular understanding of financial success as the lens through which ministry success is defined at Suburban Church. The drive for this success is the implicit motivation behind the church's purpose. The second most important force is the lifestyles of suburban families and single people. Suburban Church remains one of many options from which people choose as they construct their monthly calendars. The church does not provide a meaningful alternative to the secular message about success, nor does it provide an alternative to other area programs that exist for fun or personal edification. Finally, the third force is people's desire to find a haven from a busy life, which contribute to mind-sets within the ministry of Suburban Church.

With these forces in mind, group participants engage their imaginations in scenarios that could occur for Suburban Church. Their imaginative narratives incorporate ideas they have heard from other church members throughout their work.

Scenario One: In the midst of high turnover in the suburban setting, Suburban Church eliminates programs that do not address children's welfare and any other events for which volunteers are scarce. The church decides instead to become a station-along-the-way for transient single people and families whose jobs keep resulting in transfers. While caring for its long-term members, Suburban Church also offers spiritual formation opportunities for temporary attendees through short retreats and conversation groups for those who need safe spaces in which to discern their own callings for life. The church continues to provide pre-school and after-school programming, but leaves sports and entertainment events to the new, independent churches. The staff focuses on preaching, biblical education, and spiritual formation. Small groups also focus on the latter two areas, with particular attention given to the radical nature of love found in the gospel stories illustrating the great commandment. They explore how this gospel affects them in their everyday lives. Each group is invited to think about ministries that it will offer in response to God's love. The group will participate only as long as there is energy for the meetings and for the work of the identified ministry. Then they will break up and form other groups based on either spiritual questions or mutual ministry ideas. Suburban Church continues to report to its denomination but does not succumb to pressure to grow its numbers so much as to grow its spirit.

Suburban Church defines its niche as a spiritual place where the weary become replenished and the rich are challenged to learn gratitude and appropriate responses to their blessings in the world (the great commandment), instead of dwelling in entitlement and continued competition for greater secular success. The church names the risk of decreased giving and resulting staff cuts, at least initially, as people reframe their understanding of church as a place of transformation that can be highly challenging.

Scenario Two: Suburban Church begins to decline because people do not wish to commit to long-term transition. Staff and volunteers do not have the energy to do anything more than what they already do. Lower attendance signifies smaller income. Members become discouraged and increase pressure on paid staff to recruit new members. Some members leave. Eventually staff cuts are instituted and Suburban Church becomes a small church with one minister and a part-time administrative assistant, with a few loyal families still attending.

Scenario Three: The church hires more staff and pushes forward with a renewed giving campaign so that programs are sustained and evangelism efforts are enhanced. The evangelism efforts are successful enough to reach new people in the neighborhoods, particularly people with financial means, so that the church becomes more effective in offering programs that families are also responding to in the independent churches. Suburban Church sees an opportunity to compete with these other churches as the new families invite their friends to the church. The mission-outreach program focuses on "loving neighbor" theme and carries this commandment out by inviting neighbors to church.

Each scenario for Suburban Church presents a different kind of possibility. Scenario-builders return to the focal issue at this point. The first narrative addresses the focus most directly by transforming the mind-set about success and developing a niche ministry that connects with local context. This narrative has a short-term risk as the church chooses to name the malaise as a theological issue and denominational issue, namely a misguided definition of success. If Suburban Church works at redefining this entrenched notion, it may lose much of its current constituency and denominational favor. The church may also gain a new set of interested persons who see the uniqueness of the message that addresses their own dissatisfaction with the demands of secular success.

The last scenario also addresses the focus issue, but makes only incremental changes in the approach to ministry. The congregation may feel most comfortable with this narrative because it requires less effort than the first. The second scenario indicates that little effort would be put into transforming ministry outlooks. It does not align with the focal issue but identifies a realistic option for the church. Reworking the second narrative allows for a closer connection with the focal issue and builds hope for the future.

Signposts and signals from the surrounding suburban culture, the news, and global influences on work and play provide Suburban Church with inklings about how the future will unfold. Members continue their worship and discernment practices at this point, conversing about what they see emerging as God's purposes. They have opportunity to make informed choices as the signals show themselves, responding to God's call as co-creators for the future of their church community and its mission of radical love. This process invites them to adopt an ongoing ethic of inquiry that will lead the congregation into the future with eyes open and spirits ready. Suburban Church evolves into Process-Church.

Process-Church and Scenario-building

Each of the four settings, though taken from existing contexts, represents a sample of some of the variety of mainline churches represented in North America. The descriptions of these settings provide a snapshot of the issues facing particular types of churches to illustrate how an ethic of inquiry and scenario-building lead to hope for the future. This hope, previously unimagined, provides a new outlook for churches as they watch signs of the times and imagine the role of the faith community as harbinger of good news in a world of much bad news.

Attention to the unfolding future and God's work in it invites faith communities to partner with God in reinventing the church to address the brokenness in the world. Process-Church continually evolves as the future evolves, living in concert with God's intention for the world. What makes Process-Church different from institutional church is its focus on co-creation with God to illuminate the meaning of existence by bringing forth relationship based in love. The good news of hope is based in the great commandment. Process-Church particularly places itself as an organized movement capable of responding consistently and quickly to God and neighbor, living in deep awareness of its surroundings. Process-Church liberates the mainline from its emphasis on secular success and points the church toward the realm of God's choosing: wholeness and love for the world.

10

Conclusion
Engaging Tomorrow Today

We are called to be contemplatives, that is see-ers, men and women who see the coming of God.

HENRI NOUWEN[1]

The question in chapter 1, "How can the mainline church claim new life based on wholeness and love in a postmodern, globalizing world where many understandings of truth constitute faith?" continues to be an open-ended question for persons choosing to live in intentional process.

The church receives messages from the world every day about its lack of effectiveness, its inefficiency, and its hypocrisy. A declining mainline church has lost its identity in God, in whom self-esteem and prophetic voice are located. Theological cliques form, denominations split, and people either join in the fray or walk away. Fear, depression, or grim determination characterize the moods of Western mainline denominations worldwide. The church has lost its way, wandering without hope or direction in a wilderness that seems to bear no good news. Its leaders are discouraged and exhausted.

The mainline church, with its tendency to live in a modern mindset in the midst of a postmodern world, has forgotten the purpose of its life together. Christians are not meant to call people into the church so much as to call them out of the church itself, as a people freed from bondage, to spread the good news of God's love for all. Staying within structures and systems that bind Christians to private existence, speaking encoded languages and performing barren rituals guarantees that God's realm will pass by the church. The church will not recognize this realm without watching for it and being involved in it.

There exists no easy answer to this malaise, but hope does lie in the midst of this great wilderness in which the mainline church finds itself. The manifestation of this hope is not as simplistic as a "just love one another," or "pastors simply have to love their people." The hope lies in the work of re-appropriating the radical understanding of the church's call to love even in the midst of internal hostility or depression and negativity from the world. The early church grew stronger in its energy for the faith in the midst of persecution. The Constantinian church established power in the midst of royal sanction. Perhaps the radical work of the gospel in the post-Christendom era, where secular economic standards of success rule the day, will surface again through a shift in mainline focus. Process-Church lives into the future purposes of God rather than humanity, challenging secular values with the great commandment. The results of being faithful in the complex postmodern, post-Christendom, globalizing age lead the church again to a prophetic space in the margins, free to claim its voice for the sake of the persecuted, the marginalized, and the exhausted.

To remain faithful in this era, Christians need not reject the critical thinking introduced in the Enlightenment. Developing an ethic of inquiry requires critical analysis and the ability to self-assess. Theological reflection itself is an acquired skill, allowing one to step back from experience for a time to notice the presence of God in the midst of daily life. However, relying solely on critical thinking presents its own difficulties. Being ultimately reasonable devalues the impact of mystery. The complete reduction of experience by reasonable explanation negates the deeper spiritual levels of reality. Indeed, complete reliance on reason established human beings as autonomous. Faith in reason as opposed to faith in God leads to questions about the capacity for compassion, connection, and the value of experience as learning.

Process theologians embrace both reason and mystery, ordered system and chaos. The present is a point on the time and space continuum where past and future meet. In the present, one makes choices about whom one has become as thinker and relational being. History provides rootedness as well as information about success and failure in the past. God meets human beings in the present as God met human beings in the past to invite them to this current reality. God continues to lure humanity from this point to the future as co-creators. Humanity chooses how to respond to God's call. Faithful living, living with reasonable inquiry and the experience of adventure, brings together the purpose of God and the potential of humanity. Christians who co-create a future with God become God's hands in the world as extensions of Christ's church, risking ridicule and failure in secular terms. This co-creation sets Christians apart, not because of specific actions, but because of an orientation toward the hope of God's future mixed with human intent to bring about love that prevails in the midst of disinterest or hate.

Christians are called out of the institutional church to become the living body of Christ, the hope for the future in a hurting world. Their call, grounded in the great commandment, invites the world itself to form communities of radical love, caring for each other in the face of famine, war, disease, poverty, violence, discrimination, and invisibility. This unique message of love for God and neighbor transforms faith into a unique way of living. When wholeness and love exist as true focus for Christian life and work, the realm of God draws near, so near that humanity walks within it.

Process-Church allows for genuine choices about the future of Christianity as the faithful participate fully in God's purpose. Process-Church requires an opening up of stereotypes and notions of church. Risk and indeed adventure characterize Process-Church life. Postmodern peoples embrace these experiences as opportunities for new life.

Claiming new life is the message Jesus brought to Jews and Gentiles. He taught and modeled what new life looked like. He healed to bring new life itself. He promised the Holy Spirit would bring new life and direction to the disciples as they were sent out to share the good news. Throughout Christian history, there have been times when the church has paid close attention to God's continual call to new life. The mainline church is at a critical juncture to do so again. God is ever-present, luring people called Christians into a new day of relational vitality, spiritual centeredness, and response to the world in love. The message is clear: claim new life, church, for the sake of humanity and for the love of God.

Appendix

Method Outline for Scenario-building

The scenario-building stage for Process-Church development begins with preparation work. Denominations and faith communities not tied to established churches also may find this process helpful.

Preparation for the Congregation

Preparation work can be modified or rearranged as is appropriate for each context. This work takes one to two years, though scenario-building groups can work concurrently after the congregation spends time addressing the first six steps. During this time, the leader/minister incorporates insights from the steps into worship, study, and prayer.

1. The leader/minister asks the congregation to face the facts about its present.
2. The leader/minister teaches skills for theological reflection by asking questions about the nature and mission of the church, initiating an ethic of inquiry.
3. The leader/minister invites the congregation to discover its internal and external assumptions based on the iceberg analogy.
4. The leader/minister invites the congregation to name its passions regarding ministry.
5. The leader/minister initiates study of the biblical texts referring to the great commandment in three gospels (as a congregation or in small groups).
6. The leader/minister describes and invites conversation about the scenario-building process as a means to address issues discussed in the first two steps.
7. The leader/minister teaches that change leads to a wilderness time for the congregation, both emotionally and in terms of direction for ministry.

8. The leader/minister invites the congregation to contribute to the work of the newly formed scenario-building group by providing feedback for their process and observations.

Preparation for the Scenario-building Group

1. The leader/minister and an external facilitator (colleague or denominational leader) choose a small group that will show discipline in the scenario-building process, committing twelve to eighteen months for meeting and conversation.
2. The facilitator explains the method and purpose of scenario-building and outlines timelines and expectations.

Scenario-building

The facilitator incorporates the preparatory work conducted by the congregation in steps one through five during congregational preparation into conversation about the role of church in the world. During each step below, the scenario-building group discusses its thoughts and findings with the congregation on a regular basis, making the process as transparent as possible. Input from the congregation in between meetings is welcome. Scenario-building begins at the point when congregational preparation indicates readiness and support. This work occurs over a twelve to eighteen month period.

1. The group names the focal issue before the local church based on the preparation work conducted by both the congregation and scenario-building group thus far.
2. The facilitator invites the group to begin research about:
   - the movement of God in the world
   - movements in the church locally, nationally, globally
   - denominational trends
   - local demographic changes
   - observations about clergy and lay leadership trends
   - the impact of post-Christendom on the influence of church in society
   - observations about current politics, social issues, and economics
   - postmodern characteristics

- news stories that make an impact on the community or nation
- other relevant information that the group decides to pursue

3. The group determines what external and internal forces lie behind the information they collect in Step Two.
4. The group ranks these forces in order of importance, giving particular attention to the top three or four.
5. The group develops three or four scenarios describing potential futures.
6. The group determines if the scenarios address the focal issue (Step One) and adjusts them accordingly.
7. The group invites the congregation to participate in an open-ended period when discernment of God's unfolding purpose begins to reveal itself in conjunction with the scenarios. Active response takes place as scenarios and the future begin to meet.

The congregation begins to see which possibilities are becoming viable for their ministry as co-creators with God and makes decisions as scenarios are adjusted as present evolves into future. They begin to respond to God's unfolding future after taking time to watch and discern for a few months. The process itself is repeated as often as needed in the life of the congregation, without concern for an ultimate ending point.

Notes

Introduction

[1]"The church" throughout this volume refers to the body of mainline (established, denominationally based Protestant) churches.

[2]Luke 4 (NRSV) tells of Jesus' temptations in the wilderness followed by his proclamation in the synagogue in Nazareth, where he states that he is present to bring good news and release to the captives, the poor, the physically challenged, and the ill. His programmatic statement for ministry signifies the focus of his message and actions will be freeing people from bondage.

[3]The great commandment is the fulfillment of the law and the motivation for all ministry, according to Jesus in Mark 12:28–32.

[4]"Wholeness" refers to spiritual, physical, and mental unity or well-being.

[5]As a professor and church consultant, I hear this question in mainline churches throughout North America and Europe each time I travel. The repetition of this question in a variety of forms has continued to shape my thinking about the future of the church for many years.

Chapter 1: Corner Church

[1]Howard Thurman, *The Search for Common Ground* (Richmond, Ind.: Friends United Press, 1986), 42.

Chapter 2: The Great Hope

[1]Barbara Brown Taylor, *Leaving Church* (San Francisco: HarperSanFrancisco, 2006), 221.

[2]See Jerry Adler, "In Search of the Spiritual," *Newsweek* (29 August/5 September 2005): 49–50, for statistics describing trends in the United States regarding church attendance. He indicates that reports of 44 percent attendance are inflated, and that attendance has declined to 20 percent of the population.

[3]Lovett H. Weems Jr., "The Lewis Center Report on Clergy Age Trends," *Lewis Center for Church Leadership,* Wesley Theological Seminary, 2006, 22. Available from www.churchleadership. com, accessed December 22, 2006.

[4]James P. Wind, "The Leadership Situation Facing American Congregations," Herndon, Va.: The Alban Institute, 2001, 6–9. Available from www.alban.org, accessed May 5, 2002.

[5]John R. Donahue, "Mark," in *HarperCollins Bible Commentary,* ed. James L. Mays (San Francisco: HarperSanFrancisco, 1988; 2000), 917.

[6]Lindsey P. Pherigo, "The Gospel According to Mark," in *The Gospels: A Commentary on Matthew, Mark, Luke, John,* ed. Charles M. Laymon (Nashville: Abingdon Press, 1983), 158.

[7]Ibid.

[8]*Temenos* is Greek for an enclosed sacred space.

[9]*Kairos* is Greek for a qualitative form of time or an opportune moment.

[10]See Exodus 16:2–3, 6–9; 17:3; Numbers 11:1, 4–6; 14:2–3; 16:13–14; 20:2–5.

[11]Exodus 4.

[12]Exodus 16:14–16; 17:5–7; Numbers 11:7–9.

[13]Mark 1:12 –13; Matthew 4:1–11; Luke 4:1–13.

[14]Genesis 1:1–10.

[15]See martyrs of the early church such as Stephen (Acts 7– 8) and Paul (Acts 9; 13; 14).

[16]See an example of United Methodist statistics in Michael Coyner, "Methodists See More No-Growth Churches," *Christian Century* (April 18, 2006): 16. Forty-three percent of 35,000 United Methodist congregations did not receive any new member by profession of faith in 2005.

[17]George G. Hunter, *Radical Outreach: The Recovery of Apostolic Ministry and Evangelism* (Nashville: Abingdon Press, 2003), 25–26.

¹⁸Parachurch organizations work outside denominations or interdenominationally, usually for evangelistic efforts (Young Life, Campus Crusade for Christ, Emmaus Walk, and Fellowship of Christian Athletes) or social action movements (homeless shelters, domestic violence response groups, and emergency aid).

¹⁹Several mainline denominations have Internet plans for church growth: see, for example, www.pcusa/org/gac/missionworkplan.htm; http://new.gbgm-umc.org/work/education/evangelism; www.ucc.org/evangelism; www.rmselca.org/connectionMar06.pdf; http://ied.gospelcom.net/church.php; and www.churchgrowth.net, accessed February 28, 2007.

²⁰From http://www.google.com/search?hl=en&q=church+Growth, accessed February 17, 2005, and February 17, 2007.

²¹Bill Torbert and Associates, *Action-Inquiry: The Secret of Timely and Transforming Leadership* (San Francisco: Berrett-Koehler, 2004), 151.

²²Nancy Tatom Ammerman, *Congregation and Community* (New Brunswick, N.J.: Rutgers University Press, 2001), 5.

²³Appreciative Inquiry is a rubric of positive questions asked to promote organizational change. For resource, see David L. Cooperrider, Diana Whitney, and Jacqueline Stavros, *Appreciative Inquiry Handbook* (Bedford Heights, Ohio: Lakeshore Communications, 2003).

²⁴Ammerman, *Congregation and Community,* 262.

²⁵See the discussion on "making disciples" in Lisa R. Withrow, "Disciples for the Future: Small Groups and Vital Faith Development," *Quarterly Review* (Summer 2003): 143–46.

²⁶I consult with local churches on a regular basis to work on strategic plans and growth concerns. Few congregations know what their mission statements say. Those that do usually do not know what the statements mean or how to live into them.

²⁷Tim Conder, *The Church in Transition: The Journey of Existing Churches in the Emerging Culture* (Grand Rapids: Zondervan, 2006), 50.

²⁸Robert Wuthnow, *I Come Away Stronger: How Small Groups Are Shaping American Religion* (Grand Rapids: William B. Eerdmans, 1994), 356.

²⁹See Howard E. Friend, *Recovering the Sacred Center: Church Renewal from the Inside Out* (Valley Forge: Judson Press, 1998) for a discussion about churches finding their "sacred centers" before focusing on renewal.

³⁰Ammerman, *Congregation and Community,* 350.

³¹Thomas Bender, as cited in ibid.

³²Ibid., 352.

³³Ibid., 344.

Chapter 3: Church in Global Context

¹Peter Singer, *One World: The Ethics of Globalization* (New Haven: Yale University Press, 2002), 196.

²John W. Riggs, *Postmodern Christianity: Doing Theology in the Contemporary World* (Harrisburg, Pa.: Trinity Press International, 2003), 137.

³Henry Chadwick, "The Early Christian Community," in *The Oxford History of Christianity,* ed. John McManners (New York: Oxford University Press, 1993), 22.

⁴See ibid., 38–52, for a summary of the early history of the Christian movement in the Mediterranean world, where Christian influences affected cities, the Jewish religion and the Roman Empire.

⁵Riggs, *Postmodern Christianity,* 137–38.

⁶Ibid., 96–97.

⁷Chadwick, "Early Christian Community," 66–69.

⁸Colin Morris, "Christian Civilization," in *The Oxford History of Christianity,* ed. John McManners (Oxford: Oxford University Press, 1990), 208.

⁹See David L. Edwards, *Christianity: The First Two Thousand Years* (New York: Orbis Books, 1997), 245–46, for examples of persecution.

¹⁰Alan Richardson, "Christendom," in *The Westminster Dictionary of Christian Theology,* ed. Alan Richardson and John Bowden (Philadelphia: Westminster Press, 1983), 94.

¹¹Douglas John Hall, *Bound and Free: A Theologian's Journey* (Minneapolis: Augsburg Fortress Press, 2003), 83.

¹²Riggs, *Postmodern Christianity,* 139.

[13]Gabriel Daly, "Modernism," in *The Westminster Dictionary of Christian Theology*, ed. Alan Richardson and John Bowden (Philadelphia: Westminster Press, 1983), 376.

[14]Ibid., 376–77.

[15]Riggs, *Postmodern Christianity*, 139.

[16]Anthony B. Robinson, *Transforming Congregational Culture* (Grand Rapids: William B. Eerdmans, 2003), 92-93.

[17]See Hall, *Bound and Free,* 83–86.

[18]Ibid.

[19]A. Wayne Schwab, "Re-Centering Congregational Life Around Members' Daily Missions," *Congregations* (Spring 2006): 35.

[20]Robinson, *Transforming Congregational Culture*, 93.

[21]Hall, *Bound and Free*, 121.

[22]See Philip Jenkins, *The Next Christendom: The Coming of Global Christianity* (Oxford: Oxford University Press, 2002), 2–3, for a discussion of statistics regarding the growing numbers of Christians in Latin America, Africa, and Asia. He extrapolates figures to claim that in 2025, there will be 2.6 billion Christians, of whom 633 million live in Africa, 640 million in Latin America, and 460 million in Asia. Europe will have 555 million and North America, 272 million.

[23]Scott Thomas, "The Global Resurgence of Religion," in *God and Globalization: Christ and Dominions,* ed. Max L. Stackhouse with Diane Obenchain, vol. 3 (Harrisburg, Pa.: Trinity Press International, 2002), 112.

[24]Rosemary Radford Ruether, *Integrating Ecofeminism, Globalization and World Religions* (New York: Rowman and Littlefield, 2005), 26.

[25]Islamic fundamentalists echo this accusation, advocating for religious values and ethics that condemn secularism.

[26]Roland Robertson, "Globalization and the Future of 'Traditional Religion,'" in *God and Globalization: Religion and the Powers of Common Life,* ed. Max L. Stackhouse with Peter J. Parish, vol. 1 (Harrisburg, Pa.: Trinity Press International, 2000), 53.

[27]Jurgen Moltmann, "The Destruction and Healing of the Earth," in *God and Globalization: The Spirit and the Modern Authorities,* ed. Max L. Stackhouse and Don S. Browning, vol. 2 (Harrisburg, Pa.: Trinity Press International, 2001), 216.

[28]The exceptions can be found when sacred texts are referenced for political leverage regarding issues such as homosexuality, abortion, and women's roles.

[29]Lester C. Thurow, "Economic Community and Social Investment," in *The Community of the Future,* ed. Frances Hesselbein, Marshall Goldsmith, Richard Beckhard, Richard F. Schubert (San Francisco: Jossey-Bass, 1998), 25.

[30]Mary McClintock Fulkerson, "Ecclesial Hybridity and Church Unity," in *The Blackwell Companion to Postmodern Theology,* ed. Graham Ward (Malden, Mass.: Blackwell, 2001, 2005), 266–67.

[31]Vincent J. Miller, *Consuming Religion* (New York: Continuum, 2004), 103.

[32]Michael Lerner and Jim Wallis are two prominent persons representing religious change-agent organizations, attempting to challenge political and media establishments through national movements. Their primary method of setting up networks is through community organizing rather than cultivating media attention. See Michael Lerner, *Spirit Matters* (Charlottesville, Va.: Hampton Roads, 2000) and Jim Wallis, *God's Politics: Why the Right Gets It Wrong and the Left Doesn't Get It* (New York: HarperOne, 2006).

[33]Nicholas Boyle, *Who Are We Now? Christian Humanism and the Global Market from Hegel to Heaney* (Notre Dame, Ind.: University of Notre Dame Press, 1998), 318; quoted in Stanley Hauerwas, "The Christian Difference," in *The Blackwell Companion to Postmodern Theology,* ed. Graham Ward (Malden, Mass.: Blackwell, 2001), 152.

[34]Ruether, *Integrating Ecofeminism,* ix.

[35]Ibid.

[36]Miller, *Consuming Religion,* 227.

[37]Richard W. Gillett, *The New Globalization: Reclaiming Lost Ground of our Christian Social Tradition* (Cleveland: Pilgrim Press, 2005), 11. See also Tina Rosenber, "The Free Trade Fix," *New York Times Magazine* (August 18, 2002), available at: http://www.unc.edu/courses/2005fall/geog/021/001/ HumanGeogFall05/rosenberg.doc; and Saskia Sassen, *Cities in a World Economy,* 2d ed. (Thousand Oaks, Calif.: Pine Forge Press, 2000) for a discussion of the impact of globalization on poor nations and poor within national economies such as China, Latin American countries, and sub-Saharan Africa, where economies are growing and numbers of people living in poverty are also growing.

[38]James L. Barksdale, "Communications Technology in Dynamic Organizational Communities," in *The Community of the Future*, 93.

[39]Peter Singer, *One World*, 197.

Chapter 4: Church in Postmodern Context

[1]Graham Ward, ed., "Where We Stand," in *The Blackwell Companion to Postmodern Theology* (Malden, Mass.: Blackwell , 2001, 2005), xii.

[2]See Robert Wuthnow, *I Come Away Stronger: How Small Groups Are Shaping American Religion* (Grand Rapids: William B. Eerdmans, 1994) for studies of small groups affiliated with parent churches but taking on lives of their own.

[3]For a discussion of the ramifications of *bricolage*, see Vincent J. Miller, *Consuming Religion* (New York: Continuum, 2004), 9, 174–78.

[4]Ibid., 174.

[5]Since 2000, more than 20 million Americans have begun exploring alternative spaces and forms for worship, including home churches, faith in the workplace, and online communities. For statistics, see Michael Alison Chandler and Arianne Aryanpur, "Going to Church by Staying at Home: Clergy-Less Living Room Services Seen as a Growing Trend," *Washington Post*, June 4, 2006, Section A, p. 12.

[6]David Van Biema and Rita Healy, "There's No Pulpit Like Home," *Time* (March 6, 2006): 46–48.

[7]http://www.cla.purdue.edu/academic/engl/theory/postmodernism/modules, accessed January 29 , 2007.

[8]Ward, "Where We Stand," xiv.

[9]Peter C. Hodgson, *Revisioning in the Church: Ecclesial Freedom in the New Paradigm* (Minneapolis: Fortress Press, 1989), 51.

[10]C. David Grant, *Thinking Through Our Faith: Theology for Twenty-First Century Christians* (Nashville: Abingdon Press, 1998), 52–56.

[11]This theological understanding of God is called Deism.

[12]Grace M. Jantzen, "On Changing the Imaginary," in *The Blackwell Companion to Postmodern Theology*, 282.

[13]Romanticism is characterized by a search for transcendence and heroism.

[14]The Victorian period is characterized by middle-class domesticity and self-sacrifice.

[15]Sandra M. Schneiders, *Religious Life in the New Millennium: Finding the Treasure—Locating Catholic Religious Life in a New Ecclesial and Cultural Context* (New York: Paulist Press, 2000), 111–17.

[16]http://en.wikipedia.org/wiki/Postmodernism, accessed February 28, 2007.

[17]Donald W. Shriver Jr., "The Taming of Mars," in *God and Globalization: Religion and the Powers of Common Life*, ed. Max L. Stackhouse with Peter J. Parish, vol. 1 (Harrisburg, Pa.: Trinity Press International, 2000), 165.

[18]Lois Schawver, "A Dictionary of Postmodern Terms," https://users.california.com/~rathbone/lexicon.htm, accessed February 28, 2007.

[19]Tim Conder, *The Church in Transition: The Journey of Existing Churches in the Emerging Culture* (Grand Rapids: Zondervan, 2006), 20.

[20]www.cla.purdue.edu/academic/engl/theory/postmodernism/modules, 17, accessed January 29, 2007.

[21]These observations appear first in Lisa Withrow, "An Ethic of Inquiry for the Future Church," *The Journal of Theology* (Summer 2006): 83–85.

[22]Walter Lowe, "Is There a Postmodern Gospel?" in *The Blackwell Companion to Postmodern Theology*, 493.

[23]Mary C. Grey, "'Escape the World or Change the World?' Prophecy and Mysticism: The Heart of the Postmodern Church," *Scottish Journal of Theology* (1997): 21.

[24]Michael Moynagh, *emergingchurch.intro* (Grand Rapids: Monarch Books, 2004), 69.

[25]Eddie Gibbs and Ryan K. Bolger, *Emerging Churches: Creating Christian Community in Postmodern Cultures* (Grand Rapids: Baker Academic, 2005), 29.

[26]See www.emergentvillage.com for the history of the Emergent church and its foci.

[27]Gibbs and Bolger, *Emerging Churches*, 175.

[28]Ibid., 181.

[29]Ibid., (quoting interviewee and emerging church leader Andrew Jones), 187.

[30]Ibid., 188–89.

[31]Ibid., 195–96.

[32]Ibid., 197.

[33]Ibid., 199–200.

[34]Ibid., 215.

[35]D.A. Carson, *Becoming Conversant with the Emerging Church* (Grand Rapids: Zondervan, 2005), 14–18.

[36]Ibid., 13.

Chapter 5: Foundations for Process-Church

[1]Parker Palmer, *The Courage to Teach* (San Francisco: Jossey-Bass, 1998), 56.

[2]Anthony B. Robinson, "This Thing Called Church: What Is It Really?" in *Congregations* (Herndon, Va.: The Alban Institute: Winter 2006), 23–26.

[3]See David A. Pailin, "Process Theology," in *The Westminster Dictionary of Theology*, ed. Alan Richardson and John Bowden (Philadelphia: Westminster Press, 1983), 468.

[4]See www.ctr4process.org for an explanation.

[5]See Robert B. Mellert, *What Is Process Theology? An Introduction to the Philosophy of Alfred North Whitehead and How It Is Being Applied to Christian Thought Today* (New York: Paulist Press, 1975), 43–50.

[6]Pailin, "Process Theology," 469.

[7]John B. Cobb and David Griffin, *Process Theology: An Introductory Exposition* (Philadelphia: Westminster John Knox Press, 1976), 41–62.

[8]For discussion, see Marjorie Hewitt Suchocki, *God, Christ, Church: A Practical Guide to Process Theology* (New York: Crossroad, 1982; 1989), 129–79.

[9]Ibid., 13.

[10]Ibid., 143.

[11]Ibid., 146.

[12]Ibid., 141.

[13]Ibid., 138.

[14]Ibid., 146–47.

[15]*Ekklesia*, defined in the Introduction.

[16]Diana Butler Bass makes the distinction between traditionalism and tradition in "Vital Signs," *Sojourners Magazine* (December 2005), available from www.sojo.net, accessed December 22, 2005.

[17]Diana Butler Bass, *The Practicing Congregation: Imagining a New Old Church*, (Herndon, Va.: The Alban Institute, 2004), 39, quoting John B. Thompson, "Tradition and Self in a Mediated World," in *Detraditionalization: Critical Reflection on Authority and Identity*, ed. Paul Heelas, Scott Lash, and Paul Morris (Oxford: Blackwell, 1996), 93.

[18]Further observations about transitional work and leadership roles will be explored in Part Three.

[19]Eric H. F. Law, *Sacred Acts, Holy Change: Faithful Diversity and Practical Transformation* (St. Louis: Chalice Press), 36.

[20]Ibid., 40.

[21]Ibid., 43.

[22]Ibid., 45.

[23]See Martin Buber, *I and Thou* (New York: Touchstone, 1970) for theological discussion of "the other."

Chapter 6: Imagining the Church of the Future

[1]Joan Chittister, *Wisdom Distilled from the Daily* (San Francisco: HarperSanFrancisco, 1991), 4–5.

[2]*Koinonia* is Greek for community, in this case Christian community or the fellowship of the Holy Spirit (2 Cor. 13:14).

[3]Jim Collins, *Good to Great and the Social Sectors* (New York: HarperCollins, 2005), 34. Collins's work here is adapted to the work of the church.

[4]See chapter 5 for a description of Eric Law's iceberg exercise.

[5]Collins, *Good to Great*, 34.

[6]Ibid., 20.

[7]Ibid., 23–31.

[8]See Peter Schwartz, *The Art of the Long View* (New York: Currency Doubleday, 1996).

[9]Ibid., 4.

[10]Ibid., 6.

[11]Denominational groups can do this work as well as local churches. Consultants can facilitate or someone familiar with the process itself can call forth peers to be in the conversation.

[12]Schwartz, *Art of the Long View*, 69.

[13]Tim Conder, *The Church in Transition: The Journey of Existing Churches in the Emerging Culture* (Grand Rapids: Zondervan, 2006), 55.

[14]Schwartz, *Art of the Long View*, 19.

[15]Ibid., 140.

[16]Adapted from Schwartz's business model, with a revision that eliminates Step Five, matrix-building.

[17]An outline of both the preparatory work and scenario-building steps can be found in the Appendix.

[18]Sample questions are provided later in the chapter.

[19]Examples of Virtual Churches can be found at www.churchoffools.com and www.virtualchurch.com; Internet; accessed 28 February 2007.

[20]Schwartz, Art of the Long View, 111–12.

[21]Robert Wuthnow, "The Challenge of Ministries for Young Adults," *The 2007 Williams Lectures,* Methodist Theological School in Ohio (February 27, 2007). The data presented in the lecture became available in Robert Wuthnow, *After the Baby Boomers: How Twenty- and Thirty-Somethings Are Shaping the Future of American Religion* (Princeton, N.J.: Princeton University Press, 2007) later the same year.

[22]Wuthnow, *The Williams Lectures*, 27 February 2007.

[23]Lovett H. Weems Jr., "The Lewis Center Report on Clergy Age Trends," *Lewis Center for Church Leadership,* Wesley Theological Seminary, 2006, 22. Available from www.churchleadership.com; Internet; accessed 22 December 2006, p. 22.

[24]Schwartz, *Art of the Long View*, 243.

[25]Ibid., 248.

Chapter 7: Living into Transition

[1]Thomas Merton, *A Search for Solitude: Pursuing the Monk's True Life*, ed. Lawrence Cunningham, vol. 3 (San Francisco: HarperSanFrancisco, 1996), 18.

[2]Bill Torbert and Associates, *Action-Inquiry: The Secret of Timely and Transforming Leadership* (San Francisco: Berrett-Koehler, 2004), 194.

[3]John B. Cobb and David Griffin, *Process Theology: An Introductory Exposition* (Philadelphia: Westminster John Knox Press, 1976), 130.

[4]Robert B. Mellert, *What Is Process Theology: An Introduction to the Philosophy of Alfred North Whitehead and How It Is Being Applied to Christian Thought Today* (New York: Paulist Press, 1975), 91–92.

[5]Ibid., 95.

[6]Ibid., 97.

[7]Margaret J. Wheatley and Myron Kellner-Rogers, "The Paradox and Promise of Community," in *The Community of the Future*, ed. Frances Hesselbein, Marshall Goldsmith, Richard Beckhard, Richard F. Schubert (San Francisco: Jossey-Bass, 1998), 12.

[8]Nancy Tatom Ammerman, *Congregation and Community* (New Brunswick, N.J.: Rutgers University Press, 2001), 309.

[9]Ibid., 321–23.

[10]Wheatley and Kellner-Rogers, "The Paradox and Promise of Community," 148.

[11]Gilbert Rendle, *Leading Change in the Congregation: Spiritual and Organizational Tools for Leaders* (Herndon, Va.: The Alban Institute, 1998), 83.

[12]Ibid., 94.

[13]John Scherer, "The Role of Chaos in the Creation of Change," *Creative Change* 12, no. 2 (Spring 1991): 19; quoted in Rendle, *Leading Change in the Congregation*, 94.

[14]See chapter 5.

[15]Rendle, *Leading Change in the Congregation*, 95.

[16]Margaret J. Wheatley, *Leadership and the New Science: Discovering Order in a Chaotic World* (San Francisco: Berrett-Koehler, 1999), 88.

[17]Ibid., 89.

[18]See Peter M. Senge, *The Fifth Discipline: The Art and Practice of the Learning Organization* (New York: Currency Doubleday, 1990), 68–92, for a discussion about systems thinking in organizations.

[19]Ibid., 69.

[20]See Rendle, *Leading Change in the Congregation*, 116, for a graph describing the emotional responses.

[21]At this point, the congregation meets the scenario-building group's process with openness and together they integrate their energy and skills to live into the future.

[22]Rendle, *Leading Change in the Congregation*, 116.

[23]Loren B. Mead, *Transforming Congregations for the Future* (Herndon, Va.: The Alban Institute, 1994), 49.

[24]See Ronald Richardson, *Creating a Healthier Church: Family Systems Theory, Leadership and Congregational Life* (Minneapolis: Augsburg Fortress Press, 1996), or Peter Steinke's *How Your Church Family Works* (Herndon, Va.: The Alban Institute, 1993) for discussions of emotional systems in congregations.

[25]Shifting understandings of conflict as negative and to be avoided to opportunity for transformation cannot be covered in the scope of this book. Richardson and Steinke rely on Bowen theory and Edwin Friedman's work to address this issue in family systems theory.

[26]See Luther K. Snow, *The Power of Asset Mapping: How Your Congregation Can Act on Its Gifts* (Herndon, Va.: The Alban Institute, 2004).

[27]Os Guinness, *Prophetic Untimeliness: A Challenge to the Idol of Relevance* (Grand Rapids: Baker Books, 2003), 56–67.

[28]Ibid., 57–58

[29]Ibid., 58.

[30]Ibid., 60–61.

[31]Ibid., 65.

[32]Ibid., 67.

[33]Roy Terry, "Becoming God's Church," *Congregations* (Fall 2005): 23–27. Terry tells a story about a church employing a marketing consultant who told congregants not to use words such as "church" or "Jesus Christ" in their flyers so that people would not be offended.

Chapter 8: Leadership and Process-Church

[1]Howard E. Friend, *Recovering the Sacred Center: Church Renewal from the Inside Out* (Valley Forge, Pa.: Judson Press, 1998), 16.

[2]Skill sets are essential elements in any discussion of leadership. Secular books provide lists of skills valuable for leadership development. The focus here is to create a holistic understanding of leadership needed for the work of creating Process-Church.

[3]See discussion in chapter 3

[4]Friend, *Recovering the Sacred Center*, 113.

[5]Lovett H. Weems, "Leadership and the Small Membership Church," *Leading Ideas* (December 6, 2006); available from www.churchleadership.com/leadingideas/leaddocs/2006/061206_article.html, accessed December 7, 2006.

[6]Bill Torbert and Associates, *Action-Inquiry: The Secret of Timely and Transforming Leadership* (San Francisco: Berrett-Koehler, 2004), 182.

[7]Ibid., 190.

[8]Ibid., 189.

[9]Ibid., 188.

[10]Paulo Freire, *Pedagogy of the Oppressed* (New York: Continuum, 2006), 104.

[11]See John D. Mayer, "Emotional Intelligence: Popular or Scientific Psychology?" *APA Monitor Online*, 30, no. 8 (September 1999); available from www.eqi.org/comp_tab.htm, accessed November 11, 2006. The article summarizes the history and development of the concept of Emotional Intelligence (initially from a 1985 dissertation written by Wayne Leon Payne) before it reached the business world.

Chapter 9: The Process Church

[1]Margaret Wheatley and Myron Kellner-Rogers, "The Paradox and Promise of Community," in *The Community of the Future,* ed. Frances Hesselbein, Marshall Goldsmith, Richard Beckhard, Richard F. Schubert (San Francisco: Jossey-Bass, 1998), 18.

[2]The Church of the Saviour in Washington, D.C., has adopted an implicit ethic of inquiry. Small groups initiate a "call for response" to poverty and injustice in the area as particular issues arise. This polycentric church structure has led to cells throughout the city responding effectively to social issues and neighborhood need. The small groups themselves are highly structured, requiring significant time and input and high levels of personal sacrifice. Despite significant impact in the community, group members often burn out and leave when they have a sense that they are giving themselves away completely. Former members claim having difficulty balancing the inner and outer life of faith while involved in this church work. Process-Church seeks to develop a balance of caring relationships and accountability without rigidity.

[3]These narratives stem from the author's experience or acquaintance with the different congregational settings, though are not necessarily churches the author has served. The intent is to describe congregational struggle to grow and then project what might happen should congregations become open to an ethic of inquiry that invites deeper analysis and theological work regarding the task of ministry together.

[4]Global and local have been coined as "glocal" in globalization ethics literature to represent the integration of global influences on local cultures. First mention of "glocal" appeared in a Japanese business meeting. For more information, see http://en.wikipedia.org/wiki/Glocalisation, accessed February 28, 2007.

[5]Robert Wuthnow, "The Challenge of Ministries for Young Adults," *The 2007 Williams Lectures,* Methodist Theological School in Ohio (February 27, 2007).

Chapter 10: Conclusion

[1]Henri Nouwen, *The Road to Peace,* ed. John Dear (Maryknoll, N.Y.: Orbis Books, 1998), 196.

Bibliography

Adler, Jerry. "In Search of the Spiritual," *Newsweek* (29 August/5 September 2005): 49–50.

Ammerman, Nancy Tatom. *Congregation and Community.* New Brunswick, N.J.: Rutgers University Press, 2001.

Armour, Michael C. and Don Browning. *Systems-Sensitive Leadership: Empowering Diversity Without Polarizing the Church.* Joplin, Mo.: College Press, 2000.

Barksdale, James L. "Communications Technology in Dynamic Organizational Communities," 93–100. In *The Community of the Future,* edited by Frances Hesselbein et al. San Francisco: Jossey-Bass, 1998.

Bass, Diana Butler, "Vital Signs," *Sojourners Magazine* (December 2005). Available from www.sojo.net, accessed December 22, 2005.

Bass, Dorothy C., ed. *Practicing Our Faith: A Way of Life for a Searching People.* San Francisco: Jossey-Bass, 1997.

——. *The Practicing Congregation: Imagining a New Old Church.* Herndon, Va.: The Alban Institute, 2004.

Bender, Thomas. *Community and Social Change in America.* New Brunswick, N.J.: Rutgers University Press, 1978.

Bennis, Warren. *Why Leaders Can't Lead: The Unconscious Conspiracy Continues.* San Francisco: Jossey-Bass, 1989.

Block, Peter. *Stewardship: Choosing Service Over Self-Interest.* San Francisco: Berrett-Koehler, 1996.

Boers, Arthur Paul. *Never Call Them Jerks.* Herndon, Va.: The Alban Institute, 1999.

Borg, Marcus, and Ross MacKenzie, eds. *God at 2000.* Harrisburg, Pa.: Morehouse, 2000.

Brueggemann, Walter. *The Bible and Postmodern Imagination.* London: SCM Press, 1993.

Buber, Martin. *I and Thou.* New York: Touchstone, 1970.

Carson, D.A. *Becoming Conversant with the Emerging Church.* Grand Rapids: Zondervan, 2005.

Chadwick, Henry. "The Early Christian Community." In *The Oxford History of Christianity*, edited by John McManners. New York: Oxford University Press, 1993.

Chandler, Michael Alison, and Arianne Aryanpur. "Going to Church by Staying at Home," *The Washington Post*, June 4, 2006, section A, p.12.

Chittister, Joan. *Wisdom Distilled from the Daily*. San Francisco: HarperCollins, 1991.

Cimino, Richard, and Don Lattin. *Shopping for Faith: American Religion in the New Millennium*. San Francisco: Jossey-Bass, 1998.

Cobb, John B., Jr., and David Griffin. *Process Theology: An Introductory Exposition*. Philadelphia: The Westminster Press, 1976.

Cobb, John B., Jr., and Jeanyne B. Slettom, eds. *The Process Perspective: Frequently Asked Questions about Process Theology*. St. Louis: Chalice Press, 2003.

Collins, Jim. *Good to Great*. New York: HarperCollins, 2001.

———. *Good to Great and the Social Sectors: A Monograph to Accompany Good to Great*. New York: HarperCollins, 2005.

Conder, Tim. *The Church in Transition: The Journey of Existing Churches in the Emerging Culture*. Grand Rapids: Zondervan, 2006.

Cox-Johnson, Susan. "What Leaders Need to Know About the Emerging Church," *Leading Ideas*. Available from www.churchleadership.com/leadingideas, accessed December 22, 2006.

Coyner, Michael, "Methodists See More No-Growth Churches," *Christian Century*, April 18, 2006, 16.

Daly, G. "Modernism." In *The Westminster Dictionary of Theology*, edited by Alan Richardson and John Bowden. Philadelphia: The Westminster Press, 1983.

Dark, David. *The Gospel According to America: A Meditation on a God-blessed, Christ-haunted Idea*. Louisville: Westminster John Knox Press, 2005.

Donahue, John R. "Mark." In *HarperCollins Bible Commentary*, edited by James L. Mays. San Francisco: HarperSanFrancisco, 1988. Revised, 2000.

Dulles, Avery, S.J. *Models of the Church*. New York: Doubleday, 1987.

Dykstra, Craig. *Growing in the Life of Faith: Education and Christian Practices.* Louisville: Geneva Press, 1999.

Eck, Diana. *A New Religious America: How a "Christian Country" Has Become the World's Most Religiously Diverse Nation.* New York: HarperCollins, 2001.

Edwards, David L. *Christianity: The First Two Thousand Years.* Maryknoll, N.Y.: Orbis Books, 1997.

Freire, Paulo. *Pedagogy of the Oppressed.* New York: Continuum, 1970. Reprint, 1993, 2006.

Freire, Paulo. *Pedagogy of the Oppressed,* translated by Myra Bergman Ramos. New York: Herder and Herder, 1970. Reprints, New York: Continuum, 1986, 1993, 2000.

Friedman, Thomas L. *The World Is Flat: A Brief History of the Twenty-First Century.* New York: Farrar, Straus and Giroux, 2005.

Friend, Howard E. *Recovering the Sacred Center: Church Renewal from the Inside Out.* Valley Forge, Pa.: Judson Press, 1998.

Fulkerson, Mary McClintock. "Ecclesial Hybridity and Church Unity," 265-279. In *The Blackwell Companion to Postmodern Theology,* edited by Graham Ward. Malden, Mass: Blackwell Press, 2001.

Gibbs, Eddie, and Ryan K. Bolger. *Emerging Churches: Creating Christian Community in Postmodern Cultures.* Grand Rapids: Baker Academic, 2005.

Gillett, Richard W. *The New Globalization: Reclaiming Lost Ground of Our Social Christian Tradition.* Cleveland: The Pilgrim Press, 2005.

Grant, C. David. *Thinking Through Our Faith: Theology for Twenty-First Century Christians.* Nashville: Abingdon Press, 1998.

Groff, Kent Ira. *The Soul of Tomorrow's Church: Weaving Spiritual Practices in Ministry Together.* Nashville: Upper Room Books, 2000.

Guder, Darrell L., ed. *Missional Church: A Vision for the Sending of the Church in North America.* Grand Rapids: William B. Eerdmans, 1999.

Guinness, Os. *Prophetic Untimeliness: A Challenge to the Idol of Relevance.* Grand Rapids: Baker Books, 2003.

Hall, Douglas John. *Bound and Free: A Theologian's Journey.* Minneapolis: Augsburg Fortress Press, 2005.

————.*The Cross in Our Context: Jesus and the Suffering World.* Minneapolis: Augsburg Fortress Press, 2003.

Hartshorne, Charles. *Omnipotence and Other Theological Mistakes.* Albany, N.Y.: State University of New York Press, 1984.

Hauerwas, Stanley. *In Good Company: The Church as Polis.* Notre Dame, Ind.: University of Notre Dame Press, 1995.

————."The Christian Difference," 144–161. In *The Blackwell Companion to Postmodern Theology,* edited by Graham Ward. Malden, Mass.: Blackwell Press, 2001.

Heifetz, Ronald A. *Leadership Without Easy Answers.* Cambridge, Mass.: The Belknap Press, 1994.

Herrington, Jim, Mike Bonem, and James H. Furr. *Leading Congregational Change: A Practical Guide for the Transformational Journey.* San Francisco: Jossey-Bass, 2000.

Hesselbein, Frances et al., eds. *The Community of the Future.* Drucker Foundation Future Series. San Francisco: Jossey-Bass, 1998.

Hodgson, Peter C. *Revisioning the Church: Ecclesial Freedom in the New Paradigm.* Minneapolis: Fortress Press, 1989.

Hunter, George G., III. *Church for the Unchurched.* Nashville: Abingdon Press, 1996.

Jantzen, Grace M. "On Changing the Imaginary," 280–293. In *The Blackwell Companion to Postmodern Theology,* edited by Graham Ward. Malden, Mass.: Blackwell Press, 2001.

Jenkins, Philip. *The Next Christendom: The Coming of Global Christianity.* Oxford: Oxford University Press, 2002.

Johnston, Graham. *Preaching to a Postmodern World: A Guide to Reading Twenty-First Century Listeners.* Grand Rapids: Baker Books, 2001.

Jones, Jeffrey. *Traveling Together: A Guide for Disciple-Forming Congregations.* Herndon, Va: The Alban Institute, 2006.

Jones, Tony. *Postmodern Youth Ministry.* Grand Rapids: Zondervan, 2001.

Keller, Ed, and Jon Berry. *The Influentials.* New York: The Free Press, 2003.

Kitchens, Jim. *The Postmodern Parish: New Ministry for a New Era.* Herndon, Va.: The Alban Institute, 2003.

Law, Eric H.F. *Sacred Acts, Holy Change: Faithful Diversity and Practical Transformation.* St. Louis: Chalice Press, 2002.

Lerner, Michael. *Spirit Matters.* Charlottesville, Va.: Hampton Roads, 2000.

Long, Thomas G. *Testimony: Talking Ourselves into Being Christian.* San Francisco: Jossey-Bass, 2004.

Lowe, Walter. "Is There a Postmodern Gospel?," 490–504. In *The Blackwell Companion to Postmodern Theology,* edited by Graham Ward. Malden, Mass.: Blackwell Press, 2001.

Mann, Alice. *Can Our Church Live? Redeveloping Congregations in Decline.* Herndon, Va.: The Alban Institute, 1989.

Maxwell, John C. *The 360° Leader: Developing Your Influence from Anywhere in the Organization.* Nashville: Thomas Nelson, 2005.

Mayer, John D. "Emotional Intelligence: Popular or Scientific Psychology?" *APA Monitor Online* 30, no. 8 (September 1999). Available from www.eqi.org/comp_tab.htm, accessed November 11, 2006.

McLaren, Brian D. *The Church on the Other Side.* Grand Rapids: Zondervan, 1998. Reprint 2000. Expanded ed., 2006.

Mead, Loren B. *Transforming Congregations for the Future.* Herndon, Va.: The Alban Institute, 1994. Reprints, 1995, 1997.

Mellert, Robert B. *What Is Process Theology? An Introduction to the Philosophy of Alfred North Whitehead and How It Is Being Applied to Christian Thought Today.* New York: Paulist Press, 1975.

Merton, Thomas. *A Search for Solitude: The Journals of Thomas Merton, 1952–1960. Vol. 3.* Edited by Lawrence S. Cunningham. San Francisco: HarperSanFrancisco, 1996.

Mesle, C. Robert. *Process Theology: A Basic Introduction.* St. Louis: Chalice Press, 1993.

Metzger, Bruce, and Roland Murphy, eds. *The New Oxford Annotated Bible with the Apocrypha.* New York: Oxford University Press, 1991.

Miller, Vincent J. *Consuming Religion: Christian Faith and Practice in a Consumer Culture.* New York: Continuum, 2004.

Moltmann, Jurgen. "The Destruction and Healing of the Earth," 166-190. In *God and Globalization: The Spirit and the Modern Authorities,* edited by Max L. Stackhouse and Don S. Browning. Vol. 2. Harrisburg, Pa.: Trinity Press International, 2001.

Moore, Laurence R. *Selling God: American Religion in the Marketplace of Culture*. New York: Oxford University Press, 1994.

Morris, Colin. "Christian Civilization," 205–242. In *The Oxford History of Christianity*, edited by John McManners. New York: Oxford University Press, 1993.

Moynagh, Michael. *Emergingchurch.intro*. Grand Rapids: Monarch Books, 2004.

Nouwen, Henri. *The Road to Peace*, edited by John Dear. Maryknoll, N.Y.: Orbis Books, 1998.

Ogden, Schubert M. "The Meaning of Christian Hope," 203–209. In *Religious Experience and Process Theology: The Pastoral Implications of a Major Modern Movement*, edited by Harry Cargas and Bernard Lee. New York: Paulist Press, 1976.

Osmer, Richard Robert. *The Teaching Ministry of Congregations*. Louisville: Westminster John Knox Press, 2005.

Pailin, David A. "Process Theology," 467–470. In *The Westminster Dictionary of Theology*, edited by Alan Richardson and John Bowden. Philadelphia: The Westminster Press, 1983.

Palmer, Parker. *The Courage to Teach*. San Francisco: Jossey-Bass, 1998.

Peters, Rebecca Todd. *In Search of the Good Life: The Ethics of Globalization*. New York: Continuum, 2004.

Peterson, Eugene M. *Christ Plays in Ten Thousand Places: A Conversation in Spiritual Theology*. Grand Rapids: William B. Eerdmans, 2005.

Pherigo, Lindsey P. "The Gospel According to Mark,"644–671. In *The Interpreter's One Volume Commentary of the Bible*, edited by George A. Buttrick and Charles M. Laymon. Nashville: Abingdon Press, 1971.

Rendle, Gilbert. *Leading Change in the Congregation: Spiritual and Organizational Tools for Leader*. Herndon, Va.: The Alban Institute, Inc., 1998.

Richardson, Alan. "Christendom," 94. In *The Westminster Dictionary of Theology*, edited by Alan Richardson and John Bowden. Philadelphia: The Westminster Press, 1983.

Richardson, Ronald W. *Creating a Healthier Church: Family Systems Theory, Leadership, and Congregational Life*. Minneapolis: Augsburg Fortress Press, 1996.

Riggs, John W. *Postmodern Christianity: Doing Theology in the Contemporary World.* Harrisburg, Pa.: Trinity Press International, 2003.

Robertson, Roland. "Globalization and the Future of 'Traditional Religion,'" 53–68. In *God and Globalization: Religion and the Powers of Common Life,* edited by Max L. Stackhouse and Peter J. Paris. Vol. 1. Harrisburg, Pa.: Trinity Press International, 2000.

Robinson, Anthony B. *Transforming Congregational Culture.* Grand Rapids: William B. Eerdmans, 2003.

———."This Thing Called Church: What Is It Really?" *Congregations,* Winter 2006, 23–26.

Rosenber, Tina. "The Free Trade Fix," *New York Times Magazine,* August 18, 2002.

Ruether, Rosemary Radford. *Integrating Ecofeminism, Globalization and World Religions.* New York: Rowman and Littlefield, 2005.

Sassen, Saskia. *Cities in a World Economy.* 2d ed. Thousand Oaks, Calif.: Pine Forge Press, 2000.

Schawver, Lois. "A Dictionary of Postmodern Terms." Available from https://users.california.com/~rathbone/lexicon.htm, accessed January 27, 2007.

Scherer, John. "The Role of Chaos in the Creation of Change," *Creative Change* 12, no. 2. (Spring 1991): 19.

Schneiders, Sandra M. *Religious Life in the New Millennium: Finding Treasure: Locating Catholic Religious Life in a New Ecclesial and Cultural Context.* New York: Paulist Press, 2000.

Schwab, A. Wayne. "Re-Centering Congregational Life Around Members' Daily Missions," *Congregations* (Spring 2006): 34–36.

Schwartz, Peter. *The Art of the Long View: Planning for the Future in an Uncertain World.* New York: Currency/Doubleday, 1991.

Senge, Peter M. *The Fifth Discipline: The Art and Practice of the Learning Organization.* New York: Currency/Doubleday, 1990.

Shawchuck, Norman and Gustave Rath. *Benchmarks of Quality in the Church.* Nashville: Abingdon Press, 1994.

Shepherd, Loraine MacKenzie. "Feminist Theologies for a Postmodern Church: Diversity, Community, and Scripture."

American University Studies, Series 7, Theology and Religion.
Vol. 219. New York: Peter Lang, 2002.

Shriver, Donald W. "The Taming of Mars," 140–183. In *God and Globalization: Religion and the Powers of Common Life,* edited by Max L. Stackhouse and Peter J. Paris. Vol. 1. Harrisburg, Pa.: Trinity Press International, 2000.

Singer, Peter. *One World: The Ethics of Globalization.* New Haven, Conn.: Yale University Press, 2002.

Snow, Luther K. *The Power of Asset-Mapping: How Your Congregation Can Act on Its Gifts.* Herndon, Va.: The Alban Institute, 2004.

Spears, Larry C., ed. *Insights on Leadership: Service, Stewardship, Spirit and Servant-Leadership.* New York: John Wiley & Sons, 1998.

Steinke, Peter. *How Your Church Family Works.* Herndon, Va.: The Alban Institute, 1993. Reprints, 1994, 1995, 1996, 1998, 1999, 2000, 2006.

Stone, Howard W., and James O. Duke. *How to Think Theologically.* Minneapolis: Augsburg Fortress Press, 1996.

Strauss, William, and Neil Howe. *Generations: The History of America's Future, 1584–2069.* New York: Quill/William and Morrow, 1991.

Suchocki, Marjorie Hewitt. *God, Christ, Church: A Practical Guide to Process Theology.* New York: Crossroad, 1982. Revised Edition, 1989.

Taylor, Barbara Brown. *Leaving Church.* San Francisco: HarperSanFrancisco, 2006.

Terry, Roy. "Becoming God's Church," *Congregations* (Fall 2005): 23–27.

Thomas, Scott. "The Global Resurgence of Religion," 110–138. In *God and Globalization: Christ and Dominions of Civilization,* edited by Max. L. Stackhouse and Diane B. Obenchain. Vol. 3. Harrisburg, Pa.: Trinity Press International, 2002.

Thompson, John B. "Tradition and Self in a Mediated World," 89–108. In *Detraditionalization: Critical Reflection on Authority and Identity,* edited by Paul Heelas, Scott Lash, and Paul Morris. Cambridge, Mass.: Blackwell Press, 1996.

Thurman, Howard. *The Search for Common Ground.* New York: Harper and Row, 1971. Reprint, Richmond, Ind.: Friends United Press, 1986.

Thurow, Lester. "Economic Community and Social Investment," 19–26. In *The Community of the Future,* edited by Frances Hesselbein et al. San Francisco: Jossey-Bass, 1998.

Torbert, Bill, and Associates. *Action-Inquiry: The Secret of Timely and Transforming Leadership.* San Francisco: Berrett-Koehler, 2004.

Tracy, David. *On Naming the Present: God Hermeneutics and Church.* Maryknoll, N.Y.: Orbis Books, 1994.

Van Biema, David, and Rita Healy, "There's No Pulpit Like Home," *Time,* March 6, 2006: 46–48.

Volf, Miroslav. *Exclusion & Embrace: A Theological Exploration of Identity, Otherness, and Reconciliation.* Nashville: Abingdon Press, 1996.

Volf, Miroslav, and William Katerberg, eds. *The Future of Hope: Christian Tradition amid Modernity and Postmodernity.* Grand Rapids: William B. Eerdmans, 2004.

Ward, Graham. "Introduction: Here We Stand," xii-xxvii. In *The Blackwell Companion to Postmodern Theology,* edited by Graham Ward. Malden, Mass.: Blackwell Press, 2001.

Weems, Lovett H., Jr. "Leadership and the Small Membership Church," *Leading Ideas* (December 6, 2006). Available from www.churchleadership.com/leadingideas/leaddocs/2006/061206_article.html, accessed December 7, 2006.

———. *The Lewis Center Report on Clergy Age Trends.* Lewis Center for Church Leadership, Wesley Theological Seminary, 2006. Available from www.churchleadership.com, accessed December 22, 2006.

Welch, Sharon. *A Feminist Ethic of Risk.* Minneapolis: Fortress Press, 1990.

Wheatley, Margaret J. *Leadership and the New Science: Discovering Order in a Chaotic World.* San Francisco: Berrett-Koehler, 1999.

Wheatley, Margaret J., and Myron Kellner-Rogers. "The Paradox and Promise of Community," 9–18. In *The Community of the Future,* edited by Frances Hesselbein et al. San Francisco: Jossey-Bass, 1998.

Wind, James P. "The Leadership Situation Facing American Congregations," Herndon, Va.: The Alban Institute, 2001. Available from www.alban.org, accessed May 5, 2002.

Withrow, Lisa R. "Disciples for the Future: Small Groups and Vital Faith Development," *Quarterly Review,* edited by Hendrik R. Pieterse (Summer 2003): 141–50.

———. "An Ethic of Inquiry for the Future Church," *Journal of Theology* (Summer 2006): 81–92.

Wogaman, J. Philip. *Christian Perspectives on Politics.* 2d ed. Louisville: Westminster John Knox Press, 2000.

Wuthnow, Robert. *Christianity in the 21ˢᵗ Century: Reflections on the Challenges Ahead.* New York: Oxford University Press, 1993.

———, ed. *I Come Away Stronger: How Small Groups Are Shaping American Religion.* Grand Rapids: William B. Eerdmans, 1994.

———. "The Challenge of Ministries for Young Adults," *2007 Williams Lecture Series,* Methodist Theological School in Ohio. February 27, 2007.

Yancey, George. *One Body One Spirit: Principles of Successful Multiracial Churches.* Downers Grove, Ill.: InterVarsity Press, 2003.

Selected Web Site Resources

Postmodernism

http://www.cla.purdue.edu/academic/engl/theory/postmodernism/modules
This site offers a set of teaching modules for the study of postmodernism.
http://en.wikipedia.org/wiki/Postmodernism
Wikipedia offers a variety of descriptions for postmodernism.
https://users.california.com/~rathbone/lexicon.htm
A dictionary of postmodern terms is housed in this site.

Globalization/Glocalization

http://en.wikipedia.org/wiki/Glocalisation

Process Theology

www.ctr4process.org

Church development resources

www.alban.org
> The Alban Institute offers practical resources for church development.

www.christianleaders.org
> This site introduces Almond Springs, an ongoing case study for the life of the church.

Emerging Church

www.shipoffools.com

www.churchoffools.com

www.virtualchurch.com

www.Solomonsporch.com

www.emergentvillage.com

www.imagodeicommunity.com

www.theooze.com

www.alternativeworship.org

www.sojo.net

CPSIA information can be obtained at www.ICGtesting.com
Printed in the USA
LVOW04s0624310814

401670LV00004B/341/P